Cruise Ship Stories
By Guy Beach
@Copyright 2013 Guy Beach 2013

About this book

If you are reading this intro, then I take it that you have an interest in cruise ships. It could be you want to work on a cruise ships, you want to or have taken a cruise, maybe you are looking for tips on cruising or maybe you just like fun stories about cruise ships. If you are interested in any of those items I just listed, then this book is for you.

Before we begin our journey, I guess I should tell you a little bit about myself and why I have written this book. For my cruise ship experience, I worked about 12 years on cruise ships around the world and 2 years working in shore side offices in Florida. I worked with 4 different cruise lines and worked as a scuba instructor/dive manager, shore excursion manager and then in the shore side offices as an IT geek, and finally a few years as an IT officer (yeah, I know, scuba instructor to computer geek, what can I say, it has been an interesting journey).

In those years there were more stories than I can remember, but I will do my best to tell the ones of interest, as well as showing how I got my job(s) on cruise ships, tips and tricks for cruising, and some inside knowledge one can only get by working on cruise ships for over a decade.
Another item before we leave port is that all these

stories are TRUE!!! One great thing about working on cruise ships is you do not need to make anything up and when you go home and tell your friends and family about your last contract on ships, the stories are endless. There are a few stories that are told second hand from extremely reliable sources, and I tell you which stories those are.

Since I did my first contract on ships and I would go home and tell my stories (usually in a bar or social atmosphere), everyone would say I should write a book as they really enjoyed my stories (and some stories I told from my good friends that I was certain were true, as I said before, there is no need to make up stories about ships after you have worked on them).

The format of this book might seem unconventional, but please remember, I am an ex-cruise ship member, not a profession writer or journalist, so please excuse any typo's or grammatical errors in this book, I will do my best to make it as error free as possible, but without an editor and the such, some errors may slip past spell and grammar checking and once again, please accept my apologies in advance.

The reason I just mentioned that the format may be unconventional is because this literary journey of cruise ships will not be one of an exact timeline or topics, that would be just too insanely difficult and actually would make the book not as interesting in my humble opinion. Instead I wrote this book as if you and I were sitting at a bar somewhere (you can pick the bar, but if I had my choice, it might be at Sloppy Joe's in Key West, somewhere on Patpong street in Bangkok, or anywhere in the Mediterranean).

I will start from the beginning and how I got my first job on cruise ships and I'll go over things about ships like crew bars, on board romances, crazy things crew and passengers do, hurricanes and some wild weather, on board politics, a few controversial items like scams and kickbacks (oop's, I meant to say cruise ships 401k tax free plans), and basically everything I would tell you if we had plenty of time and an open bar tab.

As for where we will go in this book, well, it will cover my time on 17 different ships across 4 cruise lines, with locations including the Caribbean, Bermuda, Central America, (with just a touch of South America), Hawaii, Alaska, the coastal regions of the far east from Tianjin, China (that is the port closest to Beijing), down to Bali in Indonesia, to crossing the Atlantic and all over the Mediterranean so we have lots of oceans to cover here so let's get started shall we.

Photos from my working on ships can be seen on my website: www.cruiseshipstories.com
The photos can help give a visual to the stories told in this book.

When you see this icon , it means we are off onto another story.

My First Job on Ships

It all started just after I graduated from High School and went on a trip to Hawaii with my family. There I took an intro to Scuba course in Maui, Hawaii and I was hooked on Scuba diving. After returning to Southern California where I lived, I enrolled in a Scuba certification course and soon I was an official PADI certified diver at the tender age of 18.

At that time I was working as a machinist, working 12 hours a day plus half day's on Saturday, so not much time for diving (or my girlfriend), but I went diving whenever I could and spent all my extra money on Scuba gear so I could stop renting gear. During the next year, I got my certification for Advanced Diver and a Rescue Diver. You may be asking yourself what this has to do with cruise ships, but I am just laying the ground work so you have a picture on how I decided to work on cruise ships.

I had quit my job as a machinist and was going to college part time and working at a big retailer in a local mall. Not exactly the exciting life some of my friends were living at the four year college's they were going to, but I refused to go to college and have no idea what degree I really wanted and what I wanted to do in life.

There came a point where it was either go back as a machinist and make a living for the rest of my life in manufacturing, or head out into the world and find out what I wanted to do and achieve in my life, and I took the latter. I quit my job at the mall, enrolled into an accelerated course to get me to be a Dive Master and then a Scuba Instructor. A month later, a couple of thousand dollars in debt and a heck of a lot of work, I was an official PADI scuba instructor who the day after getting his certification, went back to work as a machinist to pay off my debt while I looked for a job in the Caribbean or someplace exotic like that.

For those of you reading this book for cruise ship stories, I promise they are coming soon, this section is to show what it took to get a job on a cruise ship. I did not wake up one day and decide which line or ship I would work on, it was a grueling, frustrating process that I would like to share with those looking to work on ships, as well as those who vacation on cruise ships so they can have an idea of what some crewmember did to get their job on a ship.

The year was 1990, and I was a naïve young man (a kid) looking for work on either an island in the Caribbean or on cruise ships. I'd read every Scuba Diving magazine about all the different islands to dive and listened to all the stories fellow divers told me about their dive trips around the world which helped make my decision to work somewhere in the Caribbean. Now back in 1990, there was no public internet to go or Google an address or name or any information on where to send a resume to. I had to do it the old fashion way and do some research.

I started with travel agencies and got all the brochures I could find on dive places in the Caribbean as well as cruise ships and I studied them all. Literally hundreds of phone calls were made looking for an address and name to send my resume to in the hopes of landing my dream job (what that was I was not 100% sure of, but I knew it was out there and I had to find it). So I carefully typed out my resume, had many copies made, got a photo of myself (basically a mug shot with a smile), stapled my photo to my resume and sent out about a hundred to places all over the world. You may ask why I put my photo on my resume, and that answer is simple, because at that time, it was required. During my phone calls to find out where to send my resume to, they all stated they wanted a photo as well. Now this may not fly in the corporate HR world of today, but back then, they hired you partially based partially on your looks as well as your resume. Now that might not seem fair to you, but that is the way it was, and by the way, life is not fair (no matter what your mother may have told you).

I'll spare you much of the details of my search as that could be a book in itself, but I finally decided that what I really wanted to do first, was to work on cruise ships for a year to "find myself" (go ahead and take a moment to laugh at that, as I just did when writing that). It came down to three companies who hired "divers" that worked on ships as well as on some islands the cruise lines kind of owned, I'll talk more about that later.

One night I got a call from the person who contracted the dive operations for Royal Caribbean Cruise lines at the time. He called me at 10:00PM at night Pacific Time and he was based in Miami, so it was really late there, and that threw up a red flag right away. Over the phone, he offered me a job working in Haiti on a small piece of land Royal Caribbean had leased from the Haitian government. The job entailed taking passengers snorkeling while they visited the place as well as maintaining the grounds, training and help managing the local Haitian workers. It sounded like an interesting first job as a diver, but then came the details which is where the devil seems to live.

The pay for this glamorous job was about $400 a month and I had to pay for some electricity and my food and some other items. Doing the math I found that I would be working for pretty much nothing, as well as living on an island (or at least that part of the island) that practiced voodoo and who knows what. As much as I wanted to get out there and be a diver in the Caribbean, I declined the offer in the hopes that the other two options would pan out, besides, this guy seemed so desperate, I was sure I could go back and get the job as he obviously did not have many takers on his offer of paradise.

A month went by and after a few phone interviews; I received an offer to work on the Big Red Boat. For those long time cruisers out there who have not heard of that line, well, it does not exist anymore. It was a cruise line who contracted with Disney as their official cruise line and was geared toward families with small kids. The ships had Disney characters on them, and though not as plush, new and nice as the Disney cruise ships of today, it let Disney have a foothold in the cruise ship business until they built their own cruise line.

The job seemed good, the pay was ok, but the reasons I did not take it was that the line only did three and four day cruises out of Miami to 3 different ports, that's it. So it would be the same thing every week for as long as I worked there, that and the fact I would have had to dress up as a Disney character in the Bahamian heat and that did not sound fun at all. They said to call them back if I changed my mind which made me feel better that

I had a potential fall back plan if my first choice of where I wanted to work did not pan out.

During the past few months, I had also been doing some phone interviews, ok, basically it was me calling them every week to see if they had a job opening, but I'll call it interviews, with the firm that contracted the dive operations for Norwegian Cruise Lines, known as NCL. This job had most everything I wanted with the exception of actual Scuba diving. It was leading snorkeling tours, but I would learn how that can be harder at times than teaching Scuba diving, but more on that later. At first they told me I had to be a CPR and First Aid instructor as well as a Scuba Instructor to be considered for a diver position. So within a few weeks, I became a PADI Medic First Aid Instructor (which covers CPR and first aid).

Then the phone call I had been waiting for came, well kind of. One of the NCL dive managers would be at the port of Los Angeles on one of their ships there the next week and wanted to know if I could meet him for a face to face interview. So I took a Friday off of work, drove down to the port of Los Angeles, and after getting my guest pass, stepped aboard a real life cruise ship as an adult. I say as an adult because I did go on a Caribbean cruise when I was 9 years old, but I really cannot count that.

As soon as I stepped onto the gangway I knew this was the place for me. The feeling, the smell, the people, it was everything I hoped it would be and more. Ok, ok, that is abit overboard, but it really did feel like home. The shore side dive manager met me and gave me (and the two other lucky divers who were there to interview as well) a tour around the ship which I loved and we ended up at a bar to talk over the requirements of the job some more.

It was funny at the time, as we sat there at the bar, the dive manager asked if I wanted a beer. Now I was twenty years old and it was not legal for me to have a drink in the state of California, but somehow being on the ship made that law null and void, so I had a beer and we talked about the job. When he asked us for any questions, I asked him what was the number one reason divers quit the job. He thought for a moment, looked at me and said, "I lose more divers to dancers than anything else", meaning that many divers fell in love with the young hot dancers with perfect bodies (they had to be as they had to weigh in to a certain weight, some funny information on that to come soon) which sounded like a good reason as any, so the job seemed perfect to me.

The next few weeks I kept calling NCL to see if they had an opening, and when I say opening, I do not mean an actual job. You see, NCL on average interviewed 50 potential diver candidates a year on two week interviews, one week on a ship, and one week on their private island in the Bahamas. If anything it sounded like a great vacation. I would have to fly myself out to Miami and back, but they took care of most everything else. Then one summer's day I got the call that they had an opening for an interview and asked if I would like to go.

I don't think I have to tell you what I said, but to alleviate any doubt, I said yes. I'd already prepped my boss where I was working that I would need to take two weeks off without pay (I was an hourly employee with no real vacation time to go away for two weeks with pay) and they had agreed as all I ever talked about was working on cruise ships, so they knew it was my dream.

A few weeks later, I was off to Miami and the first time flying by myself. The company had me fly in the day before the ship was to board, and put me up at the Sheraton Hotel on Biscayne Bay just across from the Port of Miami. I hardly slept that night and woke up early in the morning, went outside, looked across the bay, and there it was, the ship I was going to sail on, at least for a week's interview.

There was one caveat to actually getting on the ship, and that was I had to pass some swimming tests they had that were mandatory to pass in order to be considered. If you did not pass, they sent you home right then and there, interview over! Now I had done my swimming tests for my Dive Master and Instructors certification, but that did not prepare me for this. Basically it was a free swim, then swim with masks, fins and snorkel and then running a mile. All three events had to be done within one hour from starting the first test, to completing the last.

Now I don't remember the exact lengths for the swimming part, but I can say I had to give it everything I had, but I passed with some time to spare. I found out later that about 10% of applicants fail the test and are sent home. So one more hurdle done, now it was time for my interview. Now I'm sure most people reading this book has had job interview before, but I can honestly say that till then, and until now, I never had an interview like this.

It was nonstop from six in the morning, until after midnight most of those seven days. You may be asking what I did all day and into the night, we'll, I'll tell you. I got to actually do the job I wanted, cruise ship diver and cruise staff. Wait, cruise staff you ask, I said I wanted a job as a diver, well, with one job you sometimes get another. The contract with the cruise line was to provide snorkeling tours in the ports of call, maintain staff and operations on their private island, and to also work cruise staff duties on the ships at the discretion of the cruise director.

I'll give you a list of some of the things I had to do besides taking passengers snorkeling. The lists includes; greeting passengers at the door to the nightly shows, participating in theme nights such as 50's-60's night, Caribbean night, Country Western night (which means dressing up for the theme nights in what was sometimes comical outfits), doing spotlights for the shows (I got to learn how to do professional spot lights for production shows, haven't put that on my resume yet, but it was challenging to learn), and a myriad of other things that happen during a normal day and night on a cruise ship.

All of that was on top of the actual diver job which included, selling the tours (basically saying the same speech over and over and over and over and over again) to all the passengers, getting them to sign up, helping them fill out their medical forms, manning the dive desk to sell and answer questions, working at the dive locker handing out the snorkeling gear to passengers before the snorkeling tour, actually conducting the snorkeling tours which I will speak about more later, getting all the gear back and washing it, and then conducting a farewell dive show where we would give out prizes and sign their snorkeling certificates (my tag line was, "A thousand fishes and wishes").

Now I got to do some of those things on the interview and later ended up doing all those items when I actually got the job. But back to the interview, so it was a combination of showing me what the job really entailed, how I did at selling and working with the passengers, seeing how hard I would work, and part hazing to see if I could take some verbal abuse, as well as seeing how I could hold my liquor.

Did I just say how I hold my liquor, yes I did. You see, drinking on cruise ships, especially in those days was not really an option as it was everywhere and it was not that they expected you to drink, they just knew you would and there was no way around that, so they wanted to make sure you could drink and work and keep your demeanor in public after drinking. Now we did not drink in the mornings before snorkeling tours (well, I did not at least, but that is a story for later in the book), but after the tours, or sometimes right out of the water, there could be alcohol that we helped ourselves to as we were somewhat expected. You see they wanted us to interact with the passengers, be their friends, show them a good time and the like, and that included having a drink with them.

The first night on the interview after we left the port of Miami, we did our intro show, and had probably one of the worst dinners I had ever had (which was to become the normal for me for years to come), I was then introduced to the "crew bar". Pretty much every cruise ship in the world has one of these, and many have more than one, some for crew, some for staff and some for officers. Crew/Staff/Officers are the classes on ships which I will talk about in detail throughout this book. On this ship, it was a small room that would hold about 50 people and was situated right over the propellers, so the whole room was in a state of constant vibration when at sea. Behind the small bar was usually a Pilipino bar tender whom would soon become your best friend. Back then it was 50 cent beers, and 75 cent premium drinks, and for those who smoked, a pack of cigarettes were 75 cents. Now considering all your income is disposable, as the line pays for your room, board, and food as well as a 75 dollar credit a month in the public bars on the ship, it is not a good place for those with excess issues.

So my first night ever in a crew bar consisted of Amstel Light beers and B-52 shots (Kahlua, Amaretto & Bailey's) that was for the most part, bought by the divers who worked on the ship, as well as some other crew member who would just buy me drink for what I could see, no reason except to be nice. Now I am not saying they were not nice, as I found out through my years that 99% of crew members are great people, but on this night, they had the motive of getting me drunk, and that motive was to see how I would handle it. Now even though I was 20 years old and living in a country where the legal drinking age was 21, I was no stranger to drinking, not that I drank all the time as I didn't, but it was not completely foreign to me and I will just leave it that.

For the life of me I cannot tell you how much I drank that first night, but I can tell you it was more than I have had at the parties I had gone to before. Did I say I was at a party, well the crew bar is basically Saturday night, every night of the week. I was feeling really good when I went to sleep, but not so good the next morning, but I did not complain, and did everything I was asked to do and did it with a smile on my face. Apparently that is what the cruise line was looking for, people that would just get it done no matter what and don't complain and I did my best to do just that. Some might say that cruise ship members are nothing but a group of functional drunks (not alcoholics, as drunks do not go to meetings) and to be honest, I cannot disagree with that statement.

It was a whirlwind of a week on the ship which I will tell stories from later on, but I have to say I was glad when the ship time was over and I got to go to the private island for a week. The private island is owned by Norwegian Cruise Lines (some type of thousand year land lease or something like that) and is actually called Great Stirrup Cay and is the northern most island in the Berry Islands chain in the Bahamas. For those of us who worked and lived on the island, we called it simply "The Rock". If you get a chance, Google Great Stirrup Cay and have a look at its beauty, it will help visualize what I am going to talk about here or go to my www.CruiseShipStories website where there are some photos I took while there.

Of all the places I have lived in my life, Great Stirrup Cay still goes down as my favorite. The island is 2.5 by 1.5 miles long with a nice protected cove and beach on the northern side which is where the cruise line operated. The only people who lived on the island, were about seven divers, a Norwegian caretaker who maintained the generators and machine equipment on the island, and a couple of guys who lived on the backside of the island and ran a satellite tracking station for the US military which has now been closed. The divers lived in two hundred year old house which was the old customs home on the island.

Just a little bit of history on the island, as they story went, the island was a place where back in the slave trade days, the slave ships would stop by Great Stirrup Cay and pay their tax on the slaves they were bringing to the new world. Now the slave ships captains would not want to pay tax for slaves they could not sell, so they would throw overboard those who were sick or feeble and not worth the tax they would pay on them. They would throw them in the waters between Great Stirrup Cay and Little Stirrup Cay and that bit of water became known as "Slaughter Harbor". Later on I would end up doing the best shark diving I have done in those water, I'll tell you about the fun in later on.

The cruise ships came to the island four days a week and for the three other days it was just a lonely island in the Bahamas, paradise! When the passengers were on the island, work consisted of beach duty, which was like a Bay Watch kind of thing, being a life guard, but wearing mask and snorkel slung to your waist and wearing a red snorkeling vest (snorkeling vests were mandatory on the island for guests snorkeling in the water, we wore them to set the example). There was point duty which was on spit of rock overlooking the cove where the passengers frolicked in the water and you would sit in a chair under an umbrella about twenty five feet above the water where you would sometimes have to jump into to do a rescue and help a passenger struggling to stay afloat in the water.

Then you had dive hut duty which consisted of selling snorkeling, handing out the gear, getting the gear back and cleaning it, and then there was roll on duty which was a hut on the other side of the beach where only swimming and these silly water bikes with big plastic tires were rented, those were a complete pain to maintain. So imagine a pristine beach, but with between 800 to 2000 people crowded on it, now take away the people and you are left with just the pristine beach (after the Bahamians who come over from another island to work there clean up after the messy passengers).

When everyone was gone, it was paradise on Earth. On my interview, the paradise was lost after two days when I came down with the worst sore throat I had ever had. The doctor from the ship showed up at the dive hut on the beach in his shorts and tank top and flip flops, examines me and tells me I have strep throat and that he will send over some antibiotics later that day, after he had laid out on the beach for a while to work on his tan.

My dream ended after two perfect days of working hard on the beach, doing all the chores they told me to do and loving every minute of it, my throat was killing me and the weather had turned bad. The next few days is where I learned what a "blow out" was. That is where the ship that was scheduled to stop at the island could not because of rough seas. Since the ship was my taxi ride back to Miami, that made me stuck on the island, not bad you might think, well, I had to get back to work to my real job as a machinist in

California, which meant I had to get back to Miami to catch my flight home somehow.

This is where I learned that life traveling was a journey and not the final destination and you had to roll with the changes as they happened. Since there was no ship coming to the island to take me back to Miami anytime soon, they took me on one of the islands boat, this one was a 22 foot twin engine Mako sport fisher, over to the populated island about 40 minutes hauling ass in the boat in rough seas. I walked with all my luggage (all the clothes for a week on the ship and my dive gear) to the airport. They had called ahead by VHF radio to the airport to book me a flight to Nassau.

I may have forgotten to tell you, but there was no phones on the private island, just a VHF marine radio and a single side band radio (think of a Ham radio setup). That was the first, but not last airline reservation I did using a VHF marine radio. Sitting at this tiny, and I mean tiny airport waiting for my plane to come in made me think of the Jimmy Buffet song, "No Plane on Sunday, Maybe be One Come Monday", that was the situation I was in.

Off in the distance I finally heard the hum of a plane's engines. In comes a little twin engine plane that holds eight passengers. After the passengers who were on the plane got off, I brought my stuff over to the plane when the pilot motioned me with his arm to come over. He took my luggage and tossed it (shoved it) into the little luggage compartment on the plane. I got into the seat behind where a co-pilot would sit and was feeling content that I would make it home and back to work on time.

Then some other passengers came onto the plane, next to me sat an extremely large Bahamian woman, I mean large, to this day I do not know how she fit in the seat, but she was pushing me against the side of the plane, I mean large. Ok, I thought no big deal, just a 45 minute flight to Nassau, then catch my Pan Am flight back to Miami. That is when the pilot picks up this little kid, he was about five years old I am guessing, and he hands him to the large woman next to me, and she just sets the kids right on my lap, just like that.

I look at the kid and smile and think he is just sitting there while she gets buckled in or something, but I was wrong. The pilot gets into the cockpit, having never said a word to any of us passengers and starts the engine and begins taxing down the runway while I still have this Bahamian kid sitting on my lap with no seatbelt or nothing. Not wanting to be difficult or make trouble, I just sat there with the kid on my lap the whole flight to Nassau. The flight was extremely bumpy and I found myself having to hold the kid to keep from him being tossed around the plane until we finally landed in Nassau and the plane stopped, the doors opened and the woman took the kid off my lap and left the plane, no thank you, no smile, just like that is what happened every day in the islands, and as I learned, it did happen on a normal day in the islands.

Catching my flight back to Miami without incident, I spent the night in the hotel thinking over the past two weeks which did not go exactly as planned (as I would find out thing rarely went as planned). There was no exit interview with the NCL shore side dive manager as was planned as I went straight from the airport to the hotel and thus no going over how I did on the interview with my hopefully new bosses. That night I was thinking that even though I thought I had done well on the interview; my getting strep throat might keep from getting the job. Remember that they have on average fifty interview candidates a year for maybe 15 openings during the year so any reason not to hire someone would be justification from their point of view.

Back to work in the machine shop I went, back to pulling handles and making computer and aircraft parts to pay the bills and not feeling any closer to my dream job, although the two week interview was still to this day one of the best vacations I have had, all things considered.

A few months went by with me calling NCL every week to see if there was an opening, but they just kept telling me to call back again sometime. It was not as though I expected them to hire me on the spot after my interview, but when weeks turned into months, the prospect of working on NCL ships seemed less likely with every passing day.

It was time to take life by the horns and make my own destiny, so I went down to a local dive shop in the harbor near where I lived that had recently been bought and was under new management and applied to be a Scuba Instructor. After meeting the new owner, he offered me a job teaching and working in the dive shop. The next Monday I went into my job and gave them my two weeks' notice. I was sure it was foolish thing to do as the money was good at the machine shop and it had benefits, this new job would be lots of work, with not so much pay, no benefits, but at least I would be diving and teaching which is part of what I wanted to do.

Two weeks go by and I begin my new job at the dive shop in the harbor. The owner watches me for about 10 minutes while I am teaching my first Scuba class there (or anywhere for that matter), then leaves me to teaching, satisfied that I somewhat knew what I was talking about and he had other things to do besides watch me teach. I really enjoyed teaching my first weekend of Scuba students, and then came Monday to begin working in the dive shop selling Scuba gear and accessories to tourist in the harbor.

You never know how your life will change, but I still say you can make your own luck (after all, you have to actually buy a lottery ticket to win the lottery, you can't expect just to find a ticket on the street and win), and I like to think I did make my own luck in way as all I had been working for since deciding to work on cruise ships came to be. Here it was, my third day in my first job in the Scuba industry and my mom calls me at the dive shop and tells me that a man from the cruise lines calls and wants me to call him back.

My mom gave me the phone number they had given her for me to call them back, I called the number and talked to the same shore side manager I had done the pre-interview in the Port of Los Angeles with and he said he had an opening that started in three weeks and asked if I wanted it. Once again I don't have to tell you what I told him, but to make sure there is no confusion, I told him yes, I would take the job.

There is no better feeling than working really hard to get something, and get it. The feeling is much better than just being handed something with no effort on your part, so to say the least, I was ecstatic. I went into my new bosses office on my third day of work and gave him my three weeks' notice, he was not happy, but he understood as I had told him I was trying to get job on cruise ships.

So there you have it, I know this may have been somewhat long winded to get to some cruise ship stories, but I really wanted you to know how I got there so you could hopefully understand my view of what it was like to get a job (my first one, but not my last) on a cruise ship. Thank you for reading and now, onto the stories of life on cruise ships.

The Journey Begins

"You're boyfriend just went to go Fu*% my girlfriend" were the words I heard over the nice piano music playing in the Crow's Nest bar on my first ship on my first week working on cruise ships. The words were quite clear and everyone in the lounge heard it and turned their head as did I, towards the woman yelling it. The real surprise was when I realized whom the woman was yelling this to, it was the Captain of my ship, the M/S Sunward II. Apparently the Captain and Staff Captain were hitting it up on a couple of nice beautiful young Americans on a four day cruise to the Bahamas. Both Captains had not realized that the women were lovers, but that did not stop one of the girls from wanting to have some fun with an officer, the second in command (the Staff Captain), so she went off with him and her lover was not thrilled with it and wanted to make sure everyone knew, which she did. The Captain calmed her down and took her out of the lounge, we did not hear what happened after that, but knowing ships, I'm sure both Captains had some fun with the two girls.

You can check out photos of the Sunward II at www.CruiseShipStories.com

And so life on ships began and the stories began to fill up day to day, port to port, cruise to cruise. As I stated in the introduction, imagine we are sitting at a bar and we are talking about cruise ships, so once again, the stories may sound like "Once when I was at band camp", instead they will start with, "Once when I was working on the S/S Norway….." and we will jump around from topic to topic and different points in time of my working on ships.

Since I started this chapter with the Captain, I believe now is a good time to define the politics and hierarchy on ships. It breaks down to three different groups, Officers, Staff and Crew. Officer's consists of about five percent of the crew and mostly are those who deal with the actual sailing of the ship. The operations, navigation, safety and managing the maintenance of the ship. Staff were mainly the people who interacted with the passengers, like the Cruise Staff who entertain the passengers, the casino staff that took the passengers money in the casino, the musicians, the youth staff that took care of the kids and so on. The crew were those who either served the passengers, like waiters and bar staff, and those who did the actual maintenance of the ship. Overall, if you worked on a ship, you were generally referred to as the ship's crew no matter what category you were in.

There is a distinct difference between these groups and one had to learn what those were and their boundaries. First off, officers can do no wrong, they are always right, or at least that is what they want you to believe. Officers have complete reign of the ship, unlike the staff and the crew. The staff are allowed some privileges such as interacting with guest on their off time, and access to certain parts of the passengers areas like the gym, or buffet's, but the guest always comes first, you always gave up a seat, a treadmill or your place in line to a passenger, which is why even to this day, I always let other people go in front of me and I get to the back of a line, after years of doing this, it has been hard to break that habit, the ship did a good job of training me I guess.

The crew has far less privileges than the officers and staff. They mostly cannot go into passenger areas when not on duty, and cannot go to the shows, or buffet's or passenger gym. It is obviously better to be an officer, but those jobs are few and are mainly for those in the actual business of sailing ships at sea and who went to a maritime college and who make their life at sea. Most of the jobs on ships are that of the crew, and then the staff, and then the few officers.

Remember I just said that officers are always right, well on one ship, one of my fellow divers was hitting on this passenger who also had the attention of the Chief Engineer (he runs the mechanics of the ship and report directly to the Captain). Well the Chief Engineer did not like this lowly diver cutting in on his action, so he decided that the diver's cabin door was defective and had it removed for repair, for a week. The diver had no door for a week to his cabin and the point was well known after that throughout the ship, don't get in the way of the Chief Engineer's trying to have sex with a passenger.

Now you would think Captain would have said something, and I'm sure he did with the Chief as they had some drinks, I'm sure he commended the Chief on teaching the rest of the staff and crew a lesson. Of course you may be sitting there thinking to yourself, the officer wanted to have sex with a passenger. Now that takes some explaining and I'll do my best to tell you the way it is, not the way it was supposed to be.

Back in the 1990's on ships, the rule was, "don't get caught" with a passenger. As long as there were no complaints, and there was discretion, no one would give it notice. Now get caught with a passenger in an intimate act, or if that passenger complains, well then you got fired (unless you were an officer, than it was ok). So there was risk involved if you were part of the staff or crew, and some took that risk, and some lost their jobs for it.

In today's cruise ship industry, there is a zero tolerance for having relations with a passenger and they train you relentlessly about that. As lawsuits mounted and cooperate HR took over the ships, the "look the other way" disappeared and a crew member always had to be on the defensive as some of the passengers are wanting to have sex with crew members (I say crew members as in officer, staff and crew).

A casino staff member found that out the hard way one day when a female passenger accused him of staring at her breasts and she felt harassed. At that time, the casino was wall to wall cameras, so there was documentation in the form of video surveillance of the interaction with the passenger and casino staff. From all accounts who watched the video, there was no evidence of a lewd stare or anything that could be seen on the video as offensive, but the casino staff member got fired anyway. They told him he was fired "just in case" she sued and said if she did not sue within a year, he could have his job back. Welcome to the reality of cruise ships. Most of us who worked on ships always felt like we had no rights, and in reality, we did not.

That being said, you may be asking if passengers do have sex with crew members, and the answer simply is YES. They always have and always will, that is just the reality of it. I'm sure you've seen news reports of interactions of crew and passengers and all I have to say is that a ship is a floating city, all the things that happen in a city, happen on a ship, this includes drugs, prostitution, paid protection and mafia's, yes I said mafia's, I'll go into those later.

People do stupid things, they always have and always will. For instance, two of my fellow divers back at Norwegian Cruise Lines had a three way with an eager to please passenger. How do I know this, well, I saw the photos, and I mean not on the internet like today, no this was back in the day of film cameras. These divers took a roll of film of their interlude and then had the bright idea to give the film to the ship board photographers to develop for free. Now it might not be as quick or easy without the internet, but eventually copies of the photos spread throughout the fleet and those two divers never lived it down. The divers did not get fired for it, it was just one of those "funny" incidents and then down in NCL history.

I quickly learned working on ships that when I would get to a new ship, eventually I end of at the photo lab for one reason or another, and I would always ask to see the "book". The book was prints of all the crazy photos the passengers had developed while on their cruise. The print worthy ones were mostly those with nudity and sexual behavior being shown in the photos. Now you would think that in this modern digital age, where people can take their private photos, keep them on a disk, and then print them out in the privacy of their own home, but no. Passengers still have risky photos printed, or sometimes burned to a cd as they ran out of space on the disk, and the ship board photographers were more than happy to make copies for their own viewing pleasure, something to think about before asking a ships photographer to do something with your private photos.

I had many a photographer tell me that passengers had actually asked them to photograph some intimate sessions they had with their lovers, none of those photogs said they did that, but I'm sure a few did.

Being a diver on cruise ships led to doing some tasks you may not imagine a diver doing. Like the cruise staff duties I mentioned earlier, and then there were those tasks I never would have imagined before working as a diver on ships. One example was when I was on board the M/S Seaward and they came and asked me to dive under the ships and look for drugs. Now I am not a trained drug searching diver, but that did not matter, a job needed to be done and a diver needed to do it.

This stemmed from a Carnival ship being caught in the Port of Miami with drugs attached to its hull. The scam was that in the islands, drug smugglers would dive under the ship while in port and attach drugs to the underside of the hull, then when the ship was in a US port, they would dive under and detach it and take their drugs. Usually we would dive to look for drugs in the last port before going to a US port which was good as usually the water was clear and you could do a nice clear water dive about twenty feet under the ship, look for any attached objects and you were done.

One such dive was not so pleasant as they asked me to dive to search for drugs on my ship while in the port of Miami. Now that is not clear water, but mucky with visibility of about 10 feet if you were lucky, which meant we had to get close to the hull where intakes sucking in water were and other such hazards on the underside of a ship's hull. That and the other diver I was going with told me that if I saw someone other then him, to get the hell out of there quick as they would mostly be the drug smugglers looking to retrieve their drugs and was said to have spear guns with them for obvious reasons.

That was not a relaxing dive, but I did it and thankfully during all the hull inspections I did searching for drugs I did not find any, nor any drug smugglers, but it is a fun story to tell people at a bar (like you right now, by the way, order another drink, we have a lot more stories to tell). By the way, diving under the ship was one of the few times I got paid extra for, and back then in the early 1990's, it paid $50 a dive.

A few "fun" dives I had in those early days was when the M/S Seaward lost power ship wide, including the engines when they were leaving Miami and they were still in the narrow passage of Governors Cut. I was on a ship on the West coast at the time, but heard about it the same day from my cruise director. Apparently, just as it was leaving the dock, the ship sucked up some trash into and intake and it clogged something which then triggered the ships computers that manage those systems to shut down completely so it would not get overheated. I wish I had seen it as the ship went sideways in the cut and it's bow and stern "brushed" up against the shores. They said people at the restaurant (I think it was Craw Daddies at the time) on the cut where looking up at the bow of the ship from their dining tables.

The damage was light as the bulbous bow which I have a good story about that I will tell you soon was somewhat flattened as it hit the shore and one of the propellers was slightly bent, but workable. The coast guard cleared the ship for sailing, but the damage would have to be fixed at the next dry dock which ships go to every few years for extensive maintenance you cannot do at wet dock where they do maintenance with the ship still in the water.

Four weeks later I was assigned to the M/S Seaward and I got to see the damage for myself. They had us dive the ship twice a week in ports to make sure the damage would was not getting worse. Since I had Nikonos professional underwater camera with a strobe as well an underwater video camera with an aluminum housing, they sent me down to take photos and video of the damage which paid some extra dollars. I had worked on the M/S Seaward before and knew how it sailed, but during this time, the ship shaked and shimmied when the ship was at cruising speed. It was like the thing was a vibrating bed in a hotel room and they had a lot of quarters to put in it. The ship was finally fixed at the next dry dock and still sails the seven seas today. I would end of doing hull inspections for different reasons through the next 10 plus years, but I'll get to those stories later on.

I must admit that I admire people who can think on their feet, like improv comedians, politicians and those people who get caught by the law and on the fly come up with an excuse for the act they were caught in.

While working on ships, one of the most common questions we received from a passenger is "what is the thing sticking out in front of the ship at the water". Now obviously that bit of nautical architecture has something to do with the way the ships goes through the water, but that is not an answer a passenger likes to hear. They like to hear something they can repeat to impress their friends and love ones.

Here goes the story..........One day on a cruise ship pier on a Caribbean island, myself and two other divers were walking into town, when a couple of passengers walked up to us and asked what that thingy was sticking out in front of the ship.

Having answered the question many times, I was just about to say something about its function when one of my fellow divers started to talk. He said "THAT IS A DPR", a Differential Pressure Reducer and starts to go on about how the DPR is a miracle of modern ship design. He was so good at telling this made up description, that myself and the other diver with me were listening with rapt attention to hear about this DPR.

After a few minutes, we realized that my buddy was just making all this up. The passengers listened with bated breath for this "insight" of information on cruise ship design. Soon, the passengers walked off thanking my friend for all the information. He just smiled and said it was his pleasure.

For the next 10 years and still to this day, I called the thing sticking out from the front of the ship the DPR. Once I even told a ship's Captain the story, and he loved it so much, he said he would start calling it a DPR as it sounds better than its real name, a Bulbous bow.

You can check out photos of the M/S Seaward at www.CruiseShipStories.com

One of the great things about working on ships are all the great people you get to meet from all over the world, some who work on ships and others just cruising. When I was a diver, we worked with the ship's entertainers and the guest or spotlight entertainers that would come on the ship for a cruise or two, do their shows and then head out to the next ships. Sometimes entertainers or comedians would stay for long periods of times on a ship and we would get to know them well and have some great memories and stories to share later in life.

There was one such comedian, one of my favorites to this day that we had a lot of fun with and here is a story about him. I won't say his name as I do not know if he would want to be mentioned in my book, so we will just call him a funny comedian. Well this comedian had his routine, part of which was when he would tell the audience that he would give them a choice, he would either pull a tiger from his hat, or do a simple card trick for them, it was their choice. That is when he would pull out a small Walkman cassette player, hit play and stick it up to the microphone where it would play its pre-recorded chant of "Card trick, card trick, we want the card trick", everyone would laugh and he would then proceed to do is funny card trick and the passengers loved it.

It was too much of a good opportunity to pass up, so a couple of us made a cassette tape with our own chant on it and one night we switched the tape out unknowingly to our good comedian friend. He goes on to do his bit, pulls the Walkman out, sticks it to the microphone, hits play to hear "Tiger, Tiger, we want the Tiger". Our comedic friend froze there on stage as the chant for the tiger played on throughout the lounge and he slowly turned his head to the side where we always sat and watched the show and say's into the microphone, "The crew is fu*&ing with me". He recovered and did his card trick, we had a great laugh, and we never had access to that Walkman again as he kept it with him at all times before, during and after the show.

One story which I was not there to personally witness involved this same comedian and was a legend of a story at NCL for years. Since I did not see it personally, I'll just give you the highlights. I believe it was on St. Kitts or some other tiny island in the southern Caribbean, this comedian went out scuba diving one day, ran across a baby goat, and somehow put it in his large dive bag and smuggles it on the ship. Later that night, during the Captains cocktail party, he sneaks the baby goat up to the lounge, he had put a black bow tie around its neck, and when the Captain was making his speech, he smacked the goat on the ass and it went running around the lounge like a crazy (probably just scarred) goat. The thought of the image of all those people in formal gowns and tuxedos chasing a baby goat around a lounge makes me laugh. I heard the story from those who were there, and hope that is an accurate description of the event, either way, it I a good laugh. And they could never pin it on the comedian so I was told, and he got away with it.

I suppose if I am going to mention some of the silly or some might say stupid things that people have done, I should include some of my own, and I will, starting with this one. You have heard I'm sure of people falling off the side of a cruise ship and wonder how stupid (or drunk), those people must be. Well one fine Bahamian evening after another horrible meal in the staff mess (that was the place the staff member ate, I'll tell you about ship board food later), and then some drinks in a lounge, me and my fellow crew members were on the fantail which is the back deck of the ships. It was warm and the sound of the water rustling from the propellers below us made a somewhat calming, peaceful feeling. To be honest, I cannot say who suggested it, maybe it was me, I can't remember exactly, but before I know it, I was climbing over the rail wearing my tuxedo and dress shoes, and somewhat hanging on the wrong side of the rail if you know what I mean. I do remember laughing, and how what a strange view is was being "outside the ship" so to say and looking at my friends on the deck who were laughing at us who were hanging onto the back of the ship. Then I looked down and had a great view, directly down to the white water the ships propellers were making and all of a sudden a froze like a statue, and then held onto the railing for dear life. It must have only taken me a few second to initially climb over the side, but once I realized where I was and how if I fell, I could be sucked into the propellers or something, I every so slowly crawled back over onto the deck where I could barely stand as my legs were like noodles. Everyone one was laughing except for me, I just chuckled a little and swore to myself never to do something that stupid again, and I never did, at least until I had to for my job, but that is another story for later.

Thinking of that last story reminded me of this one. When I was working on the S/S Norway as a diver, one night me and the other three divers decided to explore the ship in ways we had heard of, but never done. You see, the S/S Norway was built in 1962 and was originally the S/S France and was a transatlantic ship that held the record for a time for transatlantic crossing. It was kind of funny, my cabin had thermostat control that were still in French (froid for cold, chaud for hot), it was a charming ship and one of my favorite to this day with regards to history and lore.

Someone had written us out a hand drawn map about how to access certain areas of the ship. Now remember, this was in the early 1990's and as most critical access doors like to the engine room had locks, but there was still some old access areas that were hidden in plain sight. So we followed the map and found an access hatch next to a passenger hallway that led down to the engine room. Before you ask, we were all stone cold sober and did not have one drink before heading out on our journey, ever though it was the night before Miami and about 2:00AM. It was fun with the excitement of knowing we should not be there and could get in trouble if we were caught.

As we followed the map to the bowels of the ship, we finally found the propeller shafts. They were not as big as we thought they would be, about four feet in diameter as I can remember. We were able to walk right up to them and took pictures of each other as we leaned over the rotating shafts. Then it was off to the forward section of the ship to explore more parts of the ship. Now the S/S Norway had two huge stacks with wings on the top.

You can check out photos of the S/S Norway and its stacks at www.CruiseShipStories.com

The forward stack was no longer part of a boiler as that boiler was removed when NCL bought here as they did not need that kind of speed. So the front stack was hollow in a way with the exception of the access ladder that went all the way to the top. We climbed all the way to the top and then out onto the port (left) side wing. It had a tiny railing around it, about three inches high, so not much of a safety bar to stop you from falling far below to the outside deck. It was not the brightest thing to do, but we took photos of each other using a flash, so it was not that surprising when a security officer show his head out of the hatch and said, "Crew numbers please".

Yep, we were busted. He took our crew numbers down and we all crawled back down the inside of the funnel and back to our cabins to ponder what would happen to us. The next day we got called to the Staff Captain's office, got yelled out for doing something stupid (he did not know about us going down to the engine room though), gave us a verbal warning and said he would be contacting our shore side offices about the incident. Our shore side bosses told us it was stupid to do, but did not punish us as they had done that exact same thing when they were divers on the S/S Norway, so we got off pretty lucky overall.

There are certain lessons of life ones learns themselves, or by the life lessons of other people. I put this on in the latter. On the M/S Seaward, one of our divers, we called him Bam Bam because he looked like a grown up version of Bam Bam from the Flintstones. According to him, he had hit it off with gorgeous passenger, it was later in the evening (he was out past the 2:00AM curfew we had on the M/S Seaward) and they were in a lounge, up on stage behind the main curtain, and how shall I say this, she was on her knees in front of him and we was looking up smiling, I think you get the picture. Bam Bam said he thought he was in heaven, but after a few minutes she stopped, looked up at him from her kneeling position in front of him and asked "What's my name", to which he just stood there dumbfounded as he had no idea what her name was. She then stood up and walked away and left him standing there by himself. I think the lesson is obvious here, and I hope others can learn from Bam Bam's life lesson.

How's your drink, order another if you like and let's continue on with some more stories.

As I stated before, you do things on ships you thought you would never do in your life, one such item for me was performing in the Roaring 20's show on Norwegian Cruise Lines ships. By nature, I am an extravert if you could not tell, but that being said, I can honestly tell you that I have zero ability or talent in the performing arts or singing, or dancing (especially dancing). So it was not natural for me when they walked me through the show where I would be one of the performers.

This show was a crew show, so not a professional show and they explained all this to the audience. It was also a kind of perverted show as there was a lot of sexual innuendo and the cruise director would give a warning to the audience, basically saying, if you are a prude, then this is not for you and you should leave. It was a Roaring 20's show, so the costumes were of the 1920's where the girls would wear short red dresses with strings dangling down everywhere (we called them the car wash dress as when they would move their hips from side to side, they looked like they could wash a car if it went by them). The guys would wear black pants, white dress shirts, red bow times and a black and white striped jacket.

You can check out photos of the Roaring 20's show at www.CruiseShipStories.com

It is very difficult to give you the proper image of this show, but let me tell you a few highlights I had when doing these shows. I loved the bit where

I would run to mid stage, then a women behind me would yell stop stop, so I would stop. She then said "Your pants are coming down", I would look down and respond, "Oh no there not", and then she would reply "Oh Yes they are" as she chased after me across the stage. There you have it, that kind of sums of the show.

As a straight male, there was one fantastic bit that I enjoyed. I would dress up with just two flags stitched together with a hole for my head to come out. I just wore that and a black bikini with flames on it. Why did a straight guy like me have a black bikini with flames on it, well it was the early 1990's, I bought it and never had the guts to wear it on the beach, but somehow I had no problem going up on stage in front of a thousand people and wear it. So back to the bit, I would go up on stage to next to a female character (usually the Light House keeper) and I would say my bit that went like this, "If I were not upon the sea, someone else I'd rather be, if I were not upon the sea, a fluttering flag me (go ahead and laugh), and as you pass me by, this you'd hear me cry, blow me East, blow me West, I like lots of wind" all the while lifting the flag over my head so all could see the flame bikini I had on, and my mother called me shy when I was a kid. As I was saying the last part, I would be grabbing the breasts of the women to the left of me, and eventually when the next character came to my right, I would alternate grabbing each of their breasts.

Pervert you are probably thinking, well maybe, but it was my job. The girls would even tell me before the show to make sure I grabbed their breast with my full hand and they would grab my hands and place them on their breast, gosh I really loved my job at those moments. Then I would have some fun sometime where I would place my hands in ice (we had a cooler of free drinks back stage, imagine that), then when it was my turn, I would go out and when I grabbed the light house keepers breast, I would almost tuck my hand in her bikini that she wore and she would jump as my frozen hands touched her breasts for all to see.

Pervert you say again, but I ask you, who is worse, us who are performing these sophomoric bits, or the people doubling over laughing in the audience as we do them. The people love this on stage perversion so much, I would hear how much they loved it for the rest of the cruise.

After the show, we would run out to the doors of the theatre so we could take photos with the passengers as they left the lounge. Many wanted a photo with the flame bikini and thanks to the free drinks during the show, I would oblige. Once, an older grey haired lady tugged on my flag, pulled me toward her and she asked me, "Is that real?",

"Is what real" I replied, then she pointed to the front of my flame bikini, just shy of touching it and asked again, "Is that real?". I'm sure I turned fifty shades of red as my face got warm and I was shocked for a moment not knowing what to say. I quickly recovered, thought for a moment, then went with the moment so to speak and said to her, "Yes mam, that's 100% grade A American beef". She smiled and said, "Oh my" and walked off. My fellow cast member heard this as did the cruise director and they laughed and told everyone later in the bar about the little old lady and the American beef.

With the good, sometimes comes the not so good. The flutter flag was a great bit, but sometime bits were not so good, like when I had to be the sergeant major. He was the first on out on stage for the Upon the Sea bit and was out there the whole time as about eight more characters came out after the sergeant major, next of which was the black jack dealer. The black jack dealer would come out in a short black dress, tuxedo shirt with big balloons tucked in the shirt, which she would adjust and sometimes play with during the bit, she would stop next to the sergeant major and then say her lines of "Hit me here, hit me there, twenty one or bust (she would grab her big balloons on the or bust line), as she was saying hit me there, she would swing her right arm and hit the sergeant major in the groin and he would double over and then try and say his lines.

Safety first was the ships motto, ok, it wasn't back then, but if you were the sergeant major, you wore a sports cup in your short so when the black jack dealer hit you, it would not hurt you, but if she hit you too hard, it would hurt her hand. One evening I was the sergeant major and was a little late getting dressed from my last bit to this one. As I go out on stage, I realize I did not put my sports cup in and I panicked. As the black jack dealer walked out in front of me and then to my side, I said loud enough for her to hear, "I forgot my cup". Good I'm thinking, now she will hit me in the stomach or something, but no, I still remember the big grin on her face as she said her lines and then swung her right hand hard at my groin. I doubled over in pain, but luckily she did not hit me in the bull's eye, but she adjusted her aim on the next volley and hit me hard, I mean hard with the back of her hand right in the sweet spot on my groin and I doubled over and went down on stage. That is where I stayed for the rest of the bit while I was holding my crotch and moaning.

Later in the cruise, passengers would stop me and comment how real it looked when she hit me and how my acting was great. I just said thanks but knew there was no acting, it was all real. I never forgave the black jack dealer for that and got her back weeks later then she was the light house keeper and I was the flutter flag, I grabbed her breasts as hard as I could get away with on stage, she knew it was payback and that was the end of it.

The most memorable, or should I say, the memory I wish I could forget, was a solo with me on stage. Why in the world would they want someone who could not sing do a solo, well, read on. We did two Roaring 20's shows a night once a cruise. During the first show once, some male crew staff member did the bit of singing the song, "Let a smile be your umbrella on a rainy rainy day". Now you did not have to be good singer for this bit, but this guy hosed it bad and got booed off stage from the passengers which was the only time I ever remember them doing that.

Between shows, we ran down to the crew bar to slam some drinks in the 20 minutes we had off between the first and second show. The fad at that time was Yeager Meister shots, and we did three of them during our short break. Now add that to the six or so beers I had backstage between bits during the first show, I was feeling pretty good when showing up for show number two. That is when the cruise director got me and said I would be singing "Umbrella's" during the second show. I must have had a deer in headlights looks as I told the cruise director, "I don't know the words, I can't sing and I'm drunk". "Those are your problems, not mine" he quickly told me and ushered me off to the piano so I could sing a few bars for the piano player so he would know what key I sang in. I had no idea what bars were (besides those you drank in of course), and the only key I knew was the one to my cabin.

But as one does on ships, you just do it. So before you know it, I am going up on stage with a white wig, a frizzy short red dress on, and white sneakers as that was the only shoes I had besides my black dress shoes. I strolled up to the middle of the stage, looked out at the thousand people there, or least what I could see with two big spot lights blaring in my face, and at that moment I decided just to belt out this show tune like I was Frank Sinatra or some real singer. I can't really remember what I sounded like, but the audience seems to be loving it and I fed off their energy and for the briefest of moments, I knew what it felt like to be a singer on stage (a bad one maybe, but a singer none the less).

The moment of the performance only lasted a minute or so, as when I reached about the middle of the song, I went blank, I mean not a song lyric in my head anywhere, like a blank wall. I stood there frozen, looking at all the people who were looking with even more rasp attention as I stopped singing and they looked on to see what I would do next. The old saying goes, you stick with what you know, or in my case at this moment, what I had seen. A flash came back to me in that moment of a shore excursion manager who used to do this bit and did something at this moment during the song, and without thinking it through, I just started to do what I'd seen him do.

With no music in the background, as the band was also wondering what I was going to do, I just slightly looked to my right at some older gentlemen in the audience about 4 rows back, I looked straight forward, then glanced to my right back to him, starred him in the eye's and said this, "Stop it you savage!", to which I then stuck my tongue out as far as it would go and flicked it around at him with a sultry look. It was like I was in the audience watching myself do that and wondering to myself why in the hell I just did that. You see the cruise staff member I was referring to that did that before to the laughter of the audience was a tall flamboyant, gay black man with about the longest tongue I've ever seen, and that is not me.

Horrified with what I was doing, I was then saved by the five girls coming on stage to do the end of the bit and sing background while twirling their umbrellas. Hearing them brought the words back, and I stopped my tongue flicking and finished singing as we moved off stage to the applause of the audience. All I can say is that the cruise director never asked me to sing Umbrellas again.

During my years on ships, I would perform the, "If I were not upon the sea", on many ships, but only did the complete Roaring 20's shows on Norwegian Cruise Lines. I look back on the show with mostly great memories, but also glad I do not have to do that anymore as it was one of the toughest things I did as I had no talent for performing at all, but what I learned during that time helped me greatly as I went on and did other types of performing on ships that I will get into later on.

I know those were long stories and I hope you are still with me and not getting bored yet, so let's move on to another topic, "Gay bait". Now you know I came from Southern California in a somewhat small coastal town and until I went to ships, I don't think I had ever really knew a gay person (except for the hairdresser my mom would sometimes take me too in Los Angeles, even I knew he was gay). To be honest, gay, or homosexual never entered my mind as I am straight, to my knowledge, all my friends at the time were straight, so gay was just something you would see on TV or in the movies. The first week

I got to ships, someone told me I was "Gay Bait" and I was like, "what the hell is that". It was explained to me that because I was young, skinny and blonde, that I would be a "target" to be hit on by the gay members of the crew which were in majority in the crew staff and entertainment departments of the ship.

I'm not going to kid you, it kind of freaked me out, but this was and still is my philosophy on being "Gay Bait", and that is, I take it as a complement. When I got hit on, (and I did), I would always tell them thank you for the thought, but that I was straight. The might try and try, but homey did not play that as the saying goes. Many of my ship board friends were gay and I had some of the best times being out and about with them as they were usually hilarious to be around (except when the drama would appear, and appear it would) and us straight guys actually used the gay guys with the ladies. How in the world could you use a gay guy to get women, well it was easy. The women loved the gay guys, they loved their jokes and mannerisms and always made them and us straight guys laugh (I'll tell you about the Gay cruise later on) and we would have a great time in the bars or a club in port, and then when the evening came to an end, the gay guys would go home with their boyfriends or hook ups of the night, and us straight guys were there with the ladies who were in a great mood and did not want the night to end, so it was us straight guys or go home alone.

Ok, that is probably an overstatement of how things could go, but it did happen that way for some lucky guys. I always tell my homophobic friends that you need to worry about the day a gay guy does not hit on you, because if a gay guy won't hit on you, then what chance do you think you have the ladies. Now this all sounds like I was a "player" or something and I can tell you I was not. During this time I was just a young guy in his early 20's trying to have a good time while working, not unlike my friends were doing at the colleges they were attending.

Some of the times can be considered wild, or at least I thought back then, like when I came into the crew bar one night and 5 women grabbed me, laid me on a table, pulled my tuxedo shirt up my cummerbund down and then took turns doing shots out of my belly button for ten minutes or so, then went off on their merry way leaving me on the table with my liquor soaked belly button. I don't know why they did that, but it looked like they had a good time, and so did I.

You can check out photos of those belly shots at www.CruiseShipStories.com

There were times on Norwegian Cruise Lines when they would try to get you to be an honorary Viking by drinking 12 shots of Aquavit (made from a potato, kind of like vodka, I called it Norwegian tequila). I had a shot or two of the stuff, but was never brave (or stupid) enough to become an honorary Viking.

One thing about a diver and being on the bottom of the staff org chart is that you got an inside cabin. I only mention this as I was a little embarrassed once when I was on a ship, living in an inside cabin and I had taken a nap late in the day so I would be refreshed for my evening duties. Well, I woke up, looked at my clock and it said 7:00 and I freaked out as I had a snorkel tour going on at 7:30AM and I was never one to be late. I quickly put my dolphin shorts on, my orange dive instructor tank top, my Teva sandals, threw my snorkel gear over my shoulder and bolted out my cabin door to get to the dive locker. As I leaped into the passenger area I was quick to notice something was not right as I stood there and looked at all the passengers dressed up in their tuxedo's and dresses for formal night, and me dressed for the beach. Oops, it was 7:00PM and not 7:00AM and I was not late for anything, but a little embarrassed of my mistake, so I went back to my cabin and put on my tuxedo and went to work. This is a note for those thinking of whether to get an inside cabin or outside cabin on a cruise, unless you plan on never being in your cabin and just sleeping and showering there, get a cabin with an ocean view or balcony, preferably a balcony as it can really increase the enjoyment of your cruise, unless you fall over board which some have, I was on board on such cruise but will tell you about over board George later on in the book.

Cruise Tip: Book balcony if possible

Back in the early 1990's, no one on the ship was drug tested, except for divers of course. They introduced that due to the fact that we were about the only crew members whose job entailed passenger safety as we were responsible for them when they were in the water during a snorkeling tour. I thought it ironic that the Captain of a ship was not drug tested, but we were. At the time, I worked three months on and then two to three weeks paid vacation. Sounds great, but the reason why they did that is because the company I worked for did not want us to save up too much money and then be able to leave the job, instead you had to go on vacation every few months, pay your own travel to and from home, thus by the time vacation was over, you were out of money and had to go back to work. They would then drug test you after your vacation just before you went back to work to catch those who had too good of a time on vacation. The actual reason I mention this is because when they first started it, I was going on vacation, but after vacation I was not going to a Miami ship, but a ship out of Los Angeles and they did not have a drug test center on the West coast, so they had me take the test before leaving Miami. I was not worried about the test as I didn't and don't do drugs (besides alcohol, but luckily that is legal), but my shore side manager, the one I did my original interview offered to drive me to the test on my way to the airport as he had to take it too, great I thought.

We stopped by his apartment in Miami to drop off his things, before heading out to the medical center for the test. He had an easy way to tell people how to get to his apartment, go North on Biscayne Blvd and take a right at the first black red headed hooker you see, if you wait to the second black red headed hooker, than you have gone too far. So at his apartment he opens the frig and gets us a couple of beers which made me wonder, I mean, aren't we going to a drug test? "You have to have something to pee to take the test" he says. You have to love ships is all I thought and after a few beers it was off to pee in a cup in front of some stranger, the things you do for a job.

Nowadays drug testing is common place before you get the job and while you are employed. There are even rules now about what alcohol content you can have while on the ship, both when on duty and another when you are off duty. The only times I've seen that used is when they want to fire you, they just wait till you are drunk at a party, then go have you tested and adios, off at the next port.

Although drug testing was not common back then, drug sniffing dogs were all around, especially when going in and out of US ports. They would even bring the dogs down the crew hallways and search some cabins for drugs. I cannot remember a time when a dog came to my cabin, but I'm sure they did, it was the musicians and entertainers that always had canine visitors to their cabins and their workplace on the ship. As divers had their reputation for drinking and carousing with women, and the musicians had their reputation as pot heads and the like. We had a saying on ships that if a dog stops where your luggage is, hope he lifts his leg and takes a leak on it.

Since we are on the subject, there was a cruise years later when I was working on another cruise line that had a charter for a southern country rock music group and their fans. At the end of that cruise when we were back in the port of Miami, I had never seen so many drug sniffing dogs in my life searching through the passenger's luggage on the pier. I'd also not seen that many people being taken into rooms with an officer wearing rubber gloves, I hope they were gentle with them. I can't remember how many arrests were made that day, but it was a few to say the least, so keep that in mind when you are cruising.

Cruise Tip: Just say no to drugs – Duh!

Keeping on this topic, I do feel the need to warn people about drugs in the ports, especially Caribbean ports. DO NOT BUY DRUGS IN PORTS!!! It always amazed me at how stupid some people could be when they buy drugs from a local island guy they obviously do not know. Too many times we were in Jamaica and the ship would have to negotiate the release of a passenger who tried to buy a joint from some guy on the street. Many times it is just a scam.

Here is how it goes, you buy some drugs from a guy on the street, or maybe it was the taxi cab driver showing you around his little town and poof, you are arrested by the local island police and off to jail you go. What most did not know is that as soon as you were off to the pokey (bad choice of words I know), the drugs you bought and confiscated by the police, were given back to the guy who sold them to you and it was his brother who was the cop who busted you – get it. Then they negotiate at the police station a few thousand dollars and they will let you go and get back to your ship and of course people paid it, when they could at least.

You were lucky if they just scammed you though, there are some islands like the Cayman Islands and Bermuda, just to name two that have some fierce drug laws that they actually enforce, and no high price lawyer will get you off in those countries. There are many a crew member in Bermuda serving life in prison with no parole because they were dealing in drugs. Cayman had more a view of kicking you off the island and being black listed and never allowed to return which is much better than a third world prison I can only imagine.

When you are in the Caribbean and neighboring islands, being sold drugs is a constant thing. I remember once walking down the streets of Nassau in the Bahamas and in a matter of minutes, being offered drugs five time and I got really pissed off, first for being hassled, second for someone trying to sell me illegal stuff, homey don't play that and I was tired of it. So the next person who came up to me and whispers, "Do you want some Cocaine mon", actually he used what sounded like the word "coke", but I knew what he was selling, I then yelled out at the top of my lungs towards him, "You want to sell me cocaine", everyone turned around and in a flash the guy was gone. The funny thing is that for the rest of the day, I did get offered drugs by anyone. I guess the word had gone out about some crazy skinny white guy yelling at the drug dealers.

Drugs are not the only thing that locals are trying to sell the unwary traveler who visits their town. Prostitution is also offered in some of the more third world type islands, and I've been told that in some of those places it is legal. Luckily I do not have any stories about that (sorry for those who might have been looking forward to such stories), but I have a funny memory of Jamaica I would like to share. I was walking down the street from the ship to downtown Ocho Rios and from down this small hill covered with trees I hear a "pssssss", I stop, and look from where the sound was coming from and then I saw her. Hidden down in the hill in the foliage was an approximately 300 plus pound Jamaican woman who did not have many teeth. I won't say exactly what she spoke to me, but she was asking me if I wanted oral sex. "Yes", I said, "but not from you" and I kept walking toward town as she yelled some obscenities to me with her thick Jamaican accent.

Ocho Rios, Jamaica always made me laugh as just before you would get to town if you were coming from the old "James Bond Pier", there was a brothel on the corner that always had ladies asking you to come in. I found it odd that they were the most foul mouthed women I have ever heard, as when you politely said "NO", or just kept walking, they would cuss and swear at you and then try to talk nice to the next person that came by, got to love the islands.

On a side note, once you get to the brothel just before downtown Ocho Rios, take a right and head up the hill to a restaurant called "Evita's", it is worth the climb up the hill. To this day it is one of my favorite Italian restaurants. The baked garlic is incredible, and the jerk spaghetti is unbelievable (yes, jerk spaghetti is incredible) and the view is breath taking over the port of Ocho Rio, I highly suggest it.

Somewhat sticking to brothels in a way, I guess now is a good time to talk about Mafia's. I know you sitting there reading this and thinking of the movie the godfather, well you would be right in a way, except instead of an overweight Italian man as the god father, think of a large Pilipino, or Jamaican man. Each of the main third world ethnicities had a mafia on the ship in some form or another. And just as in life in Chicago, you do not mess with the mafia….period.

There was paid protection to prostitution to loan sharking and most of the items you would associate with a mafia. On my first ship, the cabin next to mine we all assumed was a type of brothel as it usually had 2-3 Pilipino women living in it, and a string of men going in and out of the cabin at all hours of the evening. One such evening, something must have gone wrong as a loud fight had broken out and we had no choice but to call security as it sounded like someone was getting beaten up over there. I never found out exactly what happened, but the next night it was back to the same steady flow of male crew members visiting the cabin for a short period of time.

On another ship I was on, a young beautiful Pilipino cocktail waitress was flirting with me and I was having fun flirting back somewhat, until a buddy of mine found out and informed me to stop at once, unless I wanted to marry the young lady. I was just having fun flirting, but as I was so informed, if you were to break the heart of a Pilipino, you could expect a visit from the Pilipino mafia and it could not be pretty. They take things very seriously and protect their own, even at the own expense sometimes, meaning one of the Filipino's might do something that got him fired if it would protect one of their own, you have to respect that in a way and I did and never gave a reason for a visit from the mafia.

Years later when I was working as an IT officer, I went down to fix a computer for one of the maintenance managers or something, I can't recall his exact position. Next to his computer was a wall filled with pictures of women and guns.

Having gone shooting quite a bit in my younger days, we talked about guns, he told me stories about the ladies in the photos (most of which I cannot share with you here) and I went on and fixed the issue with his computer. After I was done and was heading back to the upper decks, he told me that whenever I needed any fixed or just anything, I should call him directly, no need for a work order or anything, just call him. I shook his hand and headed up stairs and told the other IT guys how nice the man was. They just laughed and informed me that he was the current god father of the Pilipino mafia on board that ship, I just had to laugh. I never called them to fix anything as I did not want to start the "you owe me a favor" bit with the on board mafia.

On that same ship, I was having a conversion with the Captain and he started telling a few of us about one of the issues they were having with the Filipino's on board. It was a medical problem in that I doubt many businesses on land would have. The main issue was the fact that when some of the Filipino's would board the ship for their nine to twelve month contract, they would go and see the Filipino "doctor" (he was not a real doctor of course, but one of their own who would take care of what medical needs he could so they did not have to go to the actual ships doctor for various reason, here is one). The "doctor" was performing what I can only guess to be a minor surgery, you see he was implanting stainless steel ball bearings in their penis. Ok, go ahead and re-read that last sentence. Yes I said they were having ball bearings inserted into their penises.

Why you ask, well because it would make their penis bigger and what man does not want that, although the extreme that these fellows went was beyond extreme to me, but who am I to judge. So what is the issue, the issue was that because the ball bearings could set off the metal detectors in airports when the crew member was traveling ship to ship or home on vacation or back to ship, they were having these implants removed and inserted every time they left the ship and some were getting infections and other complications.

The Captain was consulting with the ship board Human Resources to discuss if they should provide them with balls made out of Teflon or some other "medical safe" material that would not set off a metal detector so they can keep their penis enlarging inserts in and not take them out. Crazy I know, but as one learns on ships, life is stranger than fiction some times. I do not know if they actually did give them some other items to insert in their penis's, only that is was a topic of discussion for the senior officers on this ship.

As much as I know you want to hear more about ball bearing filled penis's, let us move on to a more tropical subject, I would like to go back to the private island I lived on that I mentioned earlier in the book. No, I mean I really want to go back there, as I said before, it was the greatest place in the world. I realize this book is about cruise ships, but I consider the island another ship I worked on. One of the main reasons I believe the island was so magical was because when on the island, it was hard to be concerned with the issues in your life. Back then there was no internet, no phones to speak of, so you might go there and have those things in life that dominate your thoughts and worries, but since on the island there was not much you could do with regards to those issues, you just stopped worrying about them and a calm in your life takes over while there.

The worries of life off the island just became memories until you got off the island and had to face them again, that is not to say that "nothing" happened on the island, quite the contrary, stories happened. Some were of great discovery like when I went diving on an off day where the ships would anchor and were looking for any "interesting" items we might find. On this day we found the usual littered plastic cups, t-shirts and other trash one would expect to find being either tossed overboard on purpose or by accident. After about 30 minutes of diving around looking at the results of ship board litter bugs, we stumbled upon an anchor. Not just a little anchor someone lost because they did not tie off the line to the boat, this was a large anchor that looked to be off a pirate ship. It was about seven feet high and four feet wide and had been there a long time due to the growth on the anchor. The excitement was high as we raced back to the island in our small fourteen foot skiff and loaded up with rope and a large lift bag which is a bag that you can fill with air which will lift objects to the surface.

We were able to raise it after a few attempts and after a very slow troll back to the island, we placed it in the snorkeling area where passengers to this day enjoy snorkeling over the anchor that sits in about ten feet of water. It was a nice contribution to the island that has lasted for years. Other additions were not so nice so to speak.

It was one of those days on the island where there was not much to do with regards to our normal maintenance of gear and huts, so most of the guys decided to go over to the island next to us which was owned by Royal Caribbean Cruise Lines. It was the same type of island as NCL's and divers on each island would take trips to visit the others island. On this day, the guys had a little too much beer, and ended up stealing a five foot bronze statue of a pelican from RCCL's island. I was cleaning Margaretville, which was the name of our house on the island. When living on an island, there are certain things you really need to clean, like the filter on the water cooler as it fills with cockroaches that are searching for water, they get caught and drown. Disgusting I know which is why I cleaned it often. Anyway, the guys come back to the house with pelican and set him in the main room and we all take turns taking photos with the statue and laugh and think how funny it will be when the other divers found out it was missing. A few weeks went by and it kind of became part of the furniture, but was getting in the way due to its size. So someone had the great idea to sink the pelican in the snorkeling area so the passengers could enjoy it.

Wouldn't you know it, not one day after we sink the bronze bird, we get a call on the marine VHF radio from Little Stirrup Cay divers (RCCL's island) that someone shore side who was on the island noticed the statue was missing. We then found out it was a thirty thousand dollar commissioned piece of art and the divers said if it was returned immediately, they would not contact our shore side offices. Crap!, and to top it off, a storm had come onto the island and the seas were rough to say the least. Next thing you know, I am scuba diving seventeen feet in the cove attaching rope to the pelican and we are lifting it onto the boat which was much harder than dropping it overboard a few days before. We returned the bird to where it was on RCCL's island, but we did leave a noose around its neck as one last hurrah in the adventure.

As bad as a theft that may have sounded like, it was not as bad as when the RCCL divers got really drunk and attempted to steal our twenty-three foot twin engine Mako sport fisher, luckily we talked them down from that one during the theft as that one would have got ugly.

One of the draw backs to living in this paradise was that there was no hospital or medical facilities within fifty miles of the island. In the worst of cases, they would have to send out a Coast Guard helicopter to fly the wounded back to Miami. During my time there, luckily that never happened to one of our divers, although we did have some passengers get flown out, but more of that story later.

This story is one that involved alcohol and a broken neck. One of the requirements of being a diver at the time with NCL, was that you had to become an EMT (Emergency Medical Technician, which is not a paramedic, but the first step towards being one). To make is easy for us, the company would send out instructors from Broward County Community College out to the island to train us (they would do this in exchange for some free cruises). It was a packed three weeks as the training was usually done over six months. So it was work when the ships were in, then class till midnight on some days, and on days when the ship was not there, we would have class from morning till evening. Since we lived in such a remote place, they would teach us some things that were not in the normal EMT class, like giving shots.

Normally to get to the private island we go out on the Sunward II that stopped there, but the seas were rough, and the ship could not stop at the island. An executive decision was made to fly me and the EMT instructor out to the island. Now fly means, a flight from Miami to Nassau, then a flight from Nassau to Great Harbor Cay, then the divers from the private island would come and pick us up by boat to take us to the island.

Since we did not have room to pack any personal stuff (we would get our personal items when the ship was able to make it to the island), so we put our stuff wherever we could in the medical training cases. We packed up a full size resusi-ani (CPR doll) and other items needed to teach the course and headed out to the airport. Once we reached Nassau and headed to customs, that is where the fun began.

So it was our turn at the customs inspection, and the nice Bahamian lady asked us what we were doing in the Bahamas (that answer will have to wait for another story, as it is a story in itself).

She opened the resusi-ani case, and as she opened it, the look on her face made us immediately worried. After opening it all the way, we could see that there was a "white powder" all over the doll. Now it was hard enough to explain why we were traveling with a full size "female doll", but trying to explain to her about the powder, well........ it seems the instructor with me, had packed his protein shake powder in with the resusi-ani doll, and during our flight, it seemed to have exploded. So we tried to explain what the powder was and sound convincing (we were telling the truth about the powder, but sometimes even when you tell the truth, it sounds like something else).

There were a few tense moments as the agent looked at us, the doll, the powder, then around to other agents. We did not know if she was going to call for help, lock us up or what. The idea of spending time in a Bahamian jail is not a pleasant thought.

Sometimes luck is with you and the agent, who looked quite confused, finally closed the case and said "GO". We started to say something, but she said, just "GO". We took that cue to shut our mouths, grabbed our stuff, and headed out of the customs area.

Finally we made it to our island destination and I spent the next three weeks learning to be an Emergency Medical Technician.

We did have some medicine and drugs for emergencies on the island which would have to be instructed to us if necessary over VHF radio or our Single Side Band radio to use. To get on with the story, it was Halloween night and our island manager, who was already an EMT, went over to RCCL's island for a party. I distinctly remember being in the main room in our house (Margaretville), and the door opens and in walks our island manager who says to us, "Guys, I think if fu*!ed myself up".

Apparently he had come back from his evening of drinking, tied up the boat on the small dock in the cove (yeah, I know, drinking and boating) and decided to jump off the dock into the water head first. The combination of his being drunk and a low tide meant he hit his head on the bottom when he did is dive off the dock. The only good thing for him was that we had a medical instructor who was a paramedic teaching us our EMT class. We got him in, put a neck brace on him and laid him down as flat as we could. He was breathing ok, but had some loss of sensation through his body, not a very good sign, but at least he was stable.

The plan was to get him out on ship that would be in the next day, and they could take him back to Miami and if the ships onboard doctor wanted, they could request a helicopter to fly him to Miami. Well, as I've said in this book before, things don't always go as planned and this situation definitely falls into that category. The next day, the seas were rough and the Sunward II which was to be at the island "blew out" and did not stop as it could not safely tender passengers from the ship to the shore. Crap!!!

Ok, plan B, we will ask the RCCL ship (the Nordic Empress) to take him to Miami as they were scheduled to stop by their island next door and they rarely did not stop because of weather due to the protected harbor they had built, but wouldn't you know it, this is one of the few days that they did blow out. Crap Crap!!!

Onto plan C which turned out to be sending him back to Miami via airplanes using the regular airline service (if you can call it that). Now this was not a good choice, but at the time, it seemed like the best and only one we had. So we gently got him on board the Mako and headed out for Great Harbor Cay, the island next to us which had an airport (the same one I mentioned in the beginning of the book), we called on the VHF radio to the airport to make a reservation for a flight to Miami and luckily they had space and the weather was good enough for flying.

I'll never forget that trip in rough seas, as we had our island manager pushed up against the guy driving the boat at the center console, and I was on one side of him, and another diver on the other and we were holding the arm of the other guy around the manager to brace him and keep him up while bouncing in about five foot seas, not exactly what a doctor would have wanted, but we were making due.

We got him to the island and then found a man with a car that agreed to take us to the airport. Off he went in the little twin engine propeller plane to Nassau to eventually catch a flight back to Miami. When we got back on our island it was time to tell our shore side office that the island manager was on his way back to Miami. Even though we did not have cell phones or satellite phones on the island, we did have one source of communication with Miami. Every day at 10:00AM, we would call our office at the Port of Miami with our single side band radio (think of a Ham radio). At the time I was doing the calls, so I got on the microphone at 10:00AM sharp and did my "Whiskey Hotel Golf 603 this is Charley Sixer

Quebec 252" as those were our designated call signs. I informed our office that the island manager was currently on his way to Nassau and to please arrange a flight back to Miami and to pick him up at the airport and take him immediately to the hospital.

Here is where it got a little sticky as Miami was demanding to know why he was coming back to Miami. I did not want to tell them that he got drunk and did a "header" into shallow water so I told Miami that he would tell them what happened. That did not go over so well, and they were not happy with me for not telling them the details, but it was what I felt was right at the time, I gave them the information they needed at the moment, and the manager could fill them in on the details later.

He did make it to Miami and to the hospital. The doctors said that he had a broken neck and that they would need to install a "halo" to his head and secure it with bolts or something (I can't remember exactly what they had to do, but it did not sound like fun). According to the witnesses in the room at the time, the doctors asked him if he had any questions, to which he had one. He asked if he would need a catheter at any time, to which the doctor told him no, then he said, "Then I don't care what you have to do to me. This story had a happy ending as the manager fully recovered and was back at work about nine months later, he was really lucky to say the least.

Not all island stories have a happy ending like that one and here is one of those. I had just gotten off the ship and onto the island for a three month stay on the island when the night turned into one that you do not forget. The ship had left the island a few hours before and we were settling in for the night, a few of the guys were cooking dinner and I was in my bunk listening to the Black Crows album "Shake your money maker". All of sudden, the dive manager comes in and says, "Get your dive gear on, we have a search and rescue". What the hell I thought, it was dinner time and I was hungry.

On the way to the dive hut, we were informed that the Captains steward (the Filipino who attended to the Captain on the ship) was missing from the ship and his last know whereabouts was on the island. He was known to fish on the rocky side of the island and they thought he might have fallen it. So there we are diving where we found an abandoned fishing pole and a conch hammer. We searched underwater for forty minutes but did not find a trace of a body. So back to the dive hut for further instructions. The ship was back at the island by that time and they had sent some officers and men over in some lifeboats. The Sunward II was built in the early 1970's and was not what you would think of as a modern cruise ship, the life boats were just that, simple life boats, not rescue boats.

The plan was to conduct a land search around the island. As I said before, it was not a big island, but looking for a little Filipino man in the dark did not sound easy. I was tasked with getting on the Mako boat to be dropped off on the north side of the island to search for him. We had to go back to our house on the island first to fill our back packs up with beer as my dive manager told a Norwegian Officer from the ship, "You can't do a search without beer"! We got dropped off on the North side, cracked open a Heineken and started shouting "Mr. Lee, come out come out wherever you are". I know you are thinking what cruel people we were, but in what little defense I can think of, we were hungry as we did not get dinner, and we were drinking on an empty stomach. Ok, no defense at all, and it was cruel in a way, but that is the way it happened.

No luck on our search of that part of the island, so the Mako came to pick us up to take us back to the dive hut when we got a distress call from one of the life boats that was heading back to the ship to get more men for the search. Their engine had dies and they were close to the rocks on the south side. Our manager tells them over the radio to throw out their anchor and we will be there in a while to get them (we had to go back and get some more beer first). That is when they told us that they did not have an anchor on board the life boat. We all laughed upon hearing they did not have an anchor, and it was the Staff Captain on that life boat and he was not happy and embarrassed at his life boat's lack of equipment. So off we race to rescue the life boat before it ran up onto the rocks. After we hooked a tow rope to them and started to slowly make our way to the ship, my manager was looking back to them and yelling, "Its ninety dollars an hour from the time I leave the dock". He was commenting on the current rate for a tow boat in Miami where he lived and he was smiling and laughing the whole way back to the ship.

We managed to get them back to the ship and under the hooks where they could be lifted back on board the ship, all to the applause of the passengers out on deck watching us tow one of their life boats back. I'm sure those passengers did not feel that great in seeing one of their life boats being towed and wondering about the safety of the other life boats.

Back to the island to search some more (after re-stocking the beer in our back packs). We hiked to the backside of the island where we boarded our fourteen foot skiff that had repositioned to the backside to search there. We trolled along the mangroves until we found what we were looking for. Floating face down in about four feet of water was Mr. Lee, the Captains steward. Pulling alongside the body, we pulled it up and onto the boat as gently as we could, but his head ended up sliding under one of the bench seats and the ship's doctor who was with us was yelling for us to be careful as they would have to do an autopsy to determine cause of death and they did not want any injuries on him from the recovery.

The night was very quiet as we motored back to the little dock on the backside of the island. There the tractor towing a cart that took the body to the front side of the island where the Mako was waiting to take the body back to the ship. The Mako had gone out and got a body bag from the ship (yes, they have body bags on ships, and modern ships have morgues, more on that later.) and on the pier we gently put Mr. Lee in the body bag, and put him on the Mako and back to the Sunward II. As we pulled alongside the ship, passengers were out on the deck and applauding for some unknown reason, that is until we lifted up the body bag to the open hatch and the applause immediately stopped as the passengers realized what we were bringing back to the ship.

The passengers knew that the ship had returned to the island to look for the Captains steward, and it happened to be the night of the Roaring 20's show. During the show, the Captain made an announcement all over the ship, including the main lounge where the show as going and they were just starting the "If I were not upon the sea" bit. The Captain simply announced, "We have found or missing crew member, he is dead" and that was the end of the announcement. They say that many people in the lounge, including the staff members performing in the show started crying, but after a few minutes, continued with the bit as the show must go on.

As for us divers from the island, we headed back to our house overlooking the cove, heated up our now really cold dinner, and had a quiet night reflecting on what a strange evening it had been and we said a prayer for Mr. Lee.

Being an illegal alien has its ups and down. Now how in the world would a California born native know what is like to be an illegal alien, and that is simple, I was one. You see, the Bahamian immigration rules stated that a person can be in the country for up to two weeks without a work or other permit to let them stay longer. So when I was staying on the island for three months, I was there mostly as an illegal immigrant worker. Of course the Bahamian's knew we were there, but since the cruise lines paid them lots of money, and we hired people from the local islands, they looked the other way and to my knowledge, no diver was ever deported from the island.

Some of the things I look back on now are funny, but were not so at the time. One such time was on the island during the early 1990's. The first Iraq war had started, but that seemed like a distant news point that was very hard to relate to on an island with seven people, except that one of the seven was a former Navy Seal. I know what you are thinking, yeah, sure he is a Seal, but this guy was. One day when I was talking with Miami via the Single Side Band radio, they told me to have our Seal (I'll call him John), get ready to leave on the next ship back to Miami as the US Navy had called our office and wanted to speak with him.

John was not in trouble with the Navy, it was just the opposite, they wanted him to join back up and be a Seal again as they were short of trained operators at the time. He went back to Miami for a few days, and came back saying he was going back to the teams in a few weeks. He had left the Navy due to their being no room to be promoted at the time, but because of the war, they had positions available. Now John was about the nicest guy I had or have ever met. He was unassuming, meaning not a big guy, in shape but not a muscle guy. In fact you would not have given him a second look if you saw him on the street, he was just a normal guy. Then there was the story of him in Nassau where he stopped a fight using his elbows as he did not want to hurt his hands, I was not there for that, but I heard the story from about six different people, basically he was a hidden walking bad ass.

Back to the night this story is about. John was getting ready to leave the island and back in the Navy, and of course we had to throw him a party, not one party, but like a week of parties. During this time our dive manager kept asking him if he was in Grenada during the operation that took place there to free the Americans during the Regan administration. He would always just say that he could not comment on where he had been, but one night, we got some drinks into him and my manager asked if knew some bar on the beach in Grenada and then John goes on to describe the bar, so that answered that question. That night John also said one of the most poignant statements I have ever heard anyone say, he said, "Life is moments of tragedy, followed by periods of adjustment".   Think about that one for a moment.

During one of these night, Bam Bam and I decided to go for some night swimming in the cove after way too many Red Ones (cranberry and vodka) and jello shots (jello and vodka). We were jumping off "the point" into the darkness of night which was about a two story drop into the cove

below. I had just jumped and had made my way
back to the rocky shore to climb up and jump
again. I'd gotten my body about half way out of
the water and onto the rocks when something
grabbed me by the neck and pulled me back into
the water.

I dang near crapped my shorts as I flung my
arms out to get me back to the surface and there
was John with a smile on his face saying, "Sorry
about that, just trying to do a little training before
heading back". He got Bam Bam a moment later
as he dragged him down to ten feet underwater by
his feet. I don't know what happened to John after
he left NCL and went back to the teams, I hope he
is still around today being a unknown bad ass in
plain sight.

Now being a diver on the private island was
basically being a glorified life guard and you got to
take people snorkeling. As with any life guard job,
it was hours and hours of boredom, with a few
moments of action every now and then. Not all the
rescues were like in the show Bay Watch, one of
my favorite's rescues was when I was walking the
shore in the middle of the cove, when I hear and
see a wild thrashing in the water twenty five feet in
front of me out in the water. The other passengers
panicked abit and looked at me to jump in the

water (you can hear the action music in the background just like Bay Watch can't you), but I did not move and the passengers looked concerned with my "inaction" of someone drowning right in front of me. I walked a few feet into the water, cupped my hands around my mouth and shouted something, I shouted it again and the emergency was over. Wow, you must think what a great life guard I am, but please hold the applause, what I shouted was "Stand Up". After my second yell the drowning passenger heard me, put his feet down, and his six foot plus frame stood up in four feet of water. I just put a clenched fist to the top of my head which is a diver symbol for "Ok" to let the other divers in the cove who were watching that the situation was under control and then kept strolling along the beach looking for any other signs of trouble.

One rescue we had on the island tested our procedures and the outcome was somewhat comical. Near the rocky shore about half way between the beach and the point lookout, a woman started screaming at the top of her lungs and a wild thrashing in the water made her look like a violent water fountain. Not knowing what was happening, we went into rescue mode, since the point guy was closest, he dons his mask and snorkel and leaps the two story fall into the water and begins a mad swim to the victim. The diver on the beach near the shore hauls ass along the rocks to replace the point diver who had jumped in the water to cover the rest of the passengers in cove, and I ran down the beach to replace that diver near the rocks, and a diver from the hut ran down in full gear to replace me. It was poetry in motion as we all did what we had been trained to do. I started out into the water to assist the diver in the water who was now with the victim. The water was still like a fountain and the victim wailed and thrashed about. She was actually in a little yellow inner tube that we had rented to her, but that was hard to see with all the thrashing going on.

Upon getting her to shore in her tube the thrashing stopped. Expecting something terribly wrong, after getting the woman out of the inner tube we found the problem. She had been wearing one of those frilly yellow dresses that had long yellow strings dangling down from the dress. Well the Yellow Tail snapper in the cove thought she looked like a tasty treat, so out of scene from the movie Piranha, they attacked in mass at the little yellow strings and were biting her thighs and legs and she had bite marks all over her. The doctor looked her over and she was fine except for all the little fish bites on the lower part of her body.

Cruise tip: Watch out what you are wearing in the water as it may look like food to fish.

Remember I said that you can learn from the mistakes of others, here is one such lesson that I hope no one reading this would not know already, but here it goes. One fine sunny perfect Bahamian day on the island, a passenger was snorkeling in the water without the mandatory snorkel vest (that we rented if you didn't have one for ten dollars a day). So one of our divers does what we do dozens of time per day on the island and tell the passenger that he had to wear a snorkeling vest. Well he did not want to and made that vocally known to the diver and everyone within fifty feet. As it sometimes happens, the situation got heated and in short, the passenger took a swing at the diver who quickly pulled his head back to avoid the swing and as we were all watching the scene unfold, within a few seconds the passenger was surrounded by orange tank top divers. I can't remember which diver told the passenger that we can do this the easy way, or the hard way and it would be his choice. About this time a Bahamian police officer that worked the island on ship days for passenger safety (he lived on Great Harbor, the island next door) came up and told the passenger in his deep island accent that it was Bahamian law and he had to wear it. Now that is that true, but the officer was just trying to help the situation and make it easier for the man to accept wearing a snorkeling vest during his stay on the island.

Now I am going to use a word that I really don't like and would never use and don't really want this word in my book, but for the context of the story I am going to use it. Here is what happened next, the passenger looked at the dark skinned Bahamian police officer and said, "No ni$%er is going to tell me what I can't do". Upon hearing this, all of us diver stepped back as in a flash the policeman (who was carrying a pistol by the way) grabbed the guy and dragged him to a beautiful palm tree where he quickly hand cuffed the guy to the tree. And that is where the passenger stayed for about an hour or so. At least he was in the shade of the palm tree I was thinking as I always try to look at the positive side of a situation. The passenger did not say anything while handcuffed to the tree, that was the smartest thing he had done that day. Finally the officer came back, un-cuffed the passenger and told him to get back on the ship and not come back to the island, to which the passenger obeyed.

As much as I loved the island, there was only one major drawback, and that there was no women on the island, at first, some women were to come later which I will get to later on. So with no women, there was no social life of that kind on an island full of macho divers. I know that anyone reading this who has been or is in the military is right now thinking, boo hoo, poor you on a tropical island. I know, I'm just saying if the place had women, it would have been perfect. Then there were those days that put salt on the wound, like one time I was flirting with a couple of young ladies on the beach while I was on duty in the water. I had one eye on the cove for trouble, and one eye on the ladies while doing my best to be charming, then one of them said, "Can we buy you a drink tonight at the lounge", hence the salt. I then had to explain to them how I lived on the island and would not be coming back on the ship with them to which they asked if they could stay on the island tonight, ouch, more salt.

Remember I mentioned about being flown off the island in a helicopter, well here is one such time. A passenger on the beach in his fifties was having some chest pain and his chain smoking hot twenty something wife told him to go back to the ship as she still wanted to sun bathe some more. The man did as his wife said, but while on board his pains got worse and the next thing you know he is in the ships hospital where they say he needs to get to a real hospital on land as soon as possible. So on a stretcher and onto a tender to the beach where us divers are waiting for him. We have the tractor with the cart standing by to take him to the back side of the island where the helicopters pad is. The US Coast Guard was sending one of their helicopters to chopper him to Miami. So we get the guy on the cart, he had IV's and heart monitors and oxygen to help keep him stable. His beauty of a trophy wife joins us on the cart as we head to the helicopter pad. On the way there, she goes into her purse and pulls out a cigarette and begins to light it, to which I say, "Mam, we have oxygen flowing, please put out the cigarette". She looked at me with disdain and flung her cigarette out. We got the guy on the helicopter with his pissed off looking wife who seemed really upset her cruise was ending early. The next week we heard the guy had checked himself out of the hospital against medical advice, and I doubt he lasted much longer than that with that wife, I hope she was worth it.

Other times bring a smile to my face, like the time I was at the roll on hut on the other side of the beach running the silly water tricycles we rented which usually took us an hour to fix for every hour they were rented. I got a call on the radio from the dive hut for me to take the chase boat into the tender lane (where the tender that ferried people from the ship to shore and shore to ship went to access the beach), to chase a large island float we rented that had drifted into the tender lane. I told them I was busy and to send a diver in the water to do it, but they said, "Guy, trust us, you will want to do this".

As I trusted my fellow divers, I quickly swam out to the chase boat, lowered the engine and headed out to sea and then into the tender lane to see why the big round island float had wandered into the tender lane. As I approached the float I knew why the boys had wanted me to go on this task. I had been on the island for a few months, well, you know what I mean. There on the raft is a beautiful topless woman basking in the sun in all her exposed glory. Her bare breasts had little to no sag at all, even with her lying on her back, so I had to assume she was either blessed with extremely firm breasts, or they were the work of a fine plastic surgeon, but for me, I could care less, I just had a quick look (come on, who could blame me) and said, "Excuse me, mam, you need to clear the tender lane". After I yelled it out a few times, she heard me and put her top back on, smiled and waved at me and then paddles her float back to the swimming area and out of the tender lane. I guess I owed the divers for that one.

Another time I was "clearing" the beach of passengers, meaning walking around to tell them the last tender would be leaving in a few minutes back to the ship, and if they did not leave, they would have to do the dishes tonight on the island. I was moving past the roll on area of the beach, and then to sweep around the corner of the cove where it said it was ok to sun bathe topless. As I came around the corner there, lying on the beach was a beautiful woman on her towel, in a thong and nothing else. She also had her "girls" out for all the world to see, well, at least for me to see at the moment. They were obviously natural and she had a fantastic body.

I said, "excuse me" a few times, but she did not hear me as she had her earphones on and listening to her Walkman (it was the 90's remember, no mp3 players back then). Finally I walked right up to her and stood over her which blocked the sun that was shining on her glorious glistening body. With that she opened her eyes, looked up at me and gave me a big smile and removed her headphone and lifted up onto your elbows which shifted her breasts and I could not help but to smile. I told her the last tender would be leaving in a few minutes and she thanked me and put her top back on and headed back to the tender. That was a good end of the day I thought to myself.

It always amazes me how different people are. Some are not shy and show their bodies off for all the world to see, while others are just the opposite and think that the world is just trying to see them naked, which is in part true I guess, but that is human nature.

I guess it is time to leave the island and sign back on for some stories on cruise ships, order another drink and let's keep going on this voyage.

You can check out photos of Great Stirrup Cay at www.CruiseShipStories.com

As you probably are assuming, we divers had a reputation for womanizing. Actually NLC divers had a ship board reputation as womanizers, hard workers and the ones you can trust when you really needed someone. I say that in when the cruise director would need someone in a pinch to show up on time and get the job done, you called a diver as a dancer or other member of the staff might not show up or be late or something. Now I'm not saying we were better than the other staff, no way, but we worked hard and we played hard and were trusted with getting the job done which is supposed I was quite proud of.

For an example of getting the job done was in St. Thomas, I was not there for this one, but here is how the story went. A passenger had to go to the hospital with a heart problem, so divers were sent with him to escort the man to the hospital (as all divers were CPR and First Aid Instructors and most were Emergency Medical Technician's). This was on the S/S Norway which was too deep of a ship to fit into port there, so they had to take a tender to Charlotte Amalie which is the downtown area. As usual the car traffic was horrible and the ambulance they had called for was stuck on the other side of the island and this guy needed to be in a hospital as soon as possible, so the divers looked around and saw a Sparky's Liquor delivery truck and somehow managed to talk the guy into taking this sick passenger to the hospital in the back of his liquor delivery truck (imagine that, the divers choosing a liquor truck). On that cruise was one of the head executives at NCL and at the time, they were thinking of taking away the $75 a month bar allowance for divers, but after they found out how resourceful the divers were, they discarded that idea and the divers kept their bar allowance.

Of course some divers were more womanizers that others, one in particular was a real piece of work. I watched many a night at the bar when this one diver would literally go up to each single looking woman at the bar and ask her to go back to his cabin. You would think his face would hurt from being slapped all the time, but to our surprise, the women thought he was "cute" the way he asked, and more nights than not, he would hook up with a passenger by sheer determination.

One night when I was watching this diver work the bar, I heard the female passenger he was hitting on say, "I don't do one night stands", good for her I thought. And then this diver said one of the classic sleazy lines I have ever heard in my life, he looked straight at her, eye to eye and with the most cavalier smile on his face said, "This doesn't have to be a one night stand, we can write". It did not work and he went on to the next potential hookup, but I got a great laugh out of it.

I guess the reputation we had was well deserved, but in general we were also known as the "fun guys" on the ship. If you were feeling down at 2:00AM, knock on a divers door and they will get up and have a drink with you and make you feel better, that is just who we were.

After a three month stay on the private island, I was back on the Sunward II to hop a ride back to Miami to go on vacation. At dinner, I sat with a pretty young youth staff member and she asked me where I came from as she had not seen me earlier on in the cruise. I told her I was hitching a ride from the island to Miami and then she said, "Oh, you're the one". What in the world did that mean I wondered, so I asked her. She said that she and the other girls had been warned that there was a diver coming off the island from a long stay there and to watch out. Nice I thought, and I was just being nice and chatting during dinner. She then went on to tell me that before she signed onto the ship, the youth staff had a week of training in Miami and one of the questions to the youth staff was, "What is the most dangerous thing on the island", to which some said, snakes, one said sharks, but they then told them that the most dangerous thing on the island was "Divers", nice I thought again to myself, so much for being the nice guy.

The flirtatious environment was encouraged in many ways on board. On my first ship above the shore excursion tours sales desk where only crew could see was a sign that read, "Sexual harassment, its part of the benefits" and that summed up the early 1990's on ships until they got Human Resources on board after countless law suites and the like, but it was fun while it lasted.

Now in my early days on ships, the boarding passes were actually printed pieces of paper with the ships logo on it, and a space for the date of the cruise, the cabin number and what seating of dinner the people were on and all that part was hand written. That came in handy in Nassau as the shops would always hang a sign to advertise the "lucky cabin number" and if you had that cabin, you would get a hat, or bottle of booze or something. So for fun, one of the staff would go out into Nassau and find all the lucky cabin numbers and then come back to the ship with them. They would then fill out some boarding passes with those numbers on them and usually a diver and a dancer would go out into town posing as a happy couple and would go from store to store and show the vendors their boarding passes with the "lucky cabin number" on them and they would come back to the ship with bags of trinkets and booze. You can't do that today with the boarding passes now being custom printed credit cards (in more way than one), but it was one of the silly things crew members did back then to pass the time.

When most people think of cruise ships, one thing come to mind and that is the plentiful and tasty food that they have either heard about or experienced themselves on a cruise. The old cruise director joke regarding cruise ship food is, "You come on as passengers, and you disembark as cargo". Today's ship food is somewhat healthier than earlier days due to the popularity of a healthy diet, although I believe people just want to "believe" they are eating healthy, as long as it tastes good.

So back to working on ships and the food in the crew mess. When I started with Norwegian Cruise Lines, the food was absolutely, positively disgusting! The food on those ships was flavorless, swimming in oil and butter, packed with salt and was horrible for your stomach. The joke was that as soon as you signed onto the ship, you would not have a solid stool until you went on vacation. You would spend your money in port eating good food, stop by the grocery store and get frozen meals, or my favorite, spaghettios in a can and bring it back on board to eat for dinner. If you did not, then there was the always the popular yogurt and cereal dinner as they could not really mess that up.

When I would tell people I worked on cruise ships, they always wondered how I could stay so slim, it was easy, long hours of work, taking stairs all day and night to get around the ship (back then you were not allowed to use a passenger elevator, and there was maybe one or two crew elevators that were always busy, so you took the stairs), and bad tasteless food that you did not want to eat. I would tell people that we ate low grade dog food back then, and to be honest, I think dog food would have been better.

The reason the food was so bad was that they really did not care, but the actual truth was, the crew mess manager got his bonus based upon how low his food costs were. Think about that a moment, the less he spends on food for the crew, the more he gets paid, and the cruise line did not care if the crew complained. The officers generally ate what the passengers did, so the Captain and senior officers did not care of the plight of the common staff or crew.

I have to say it got better as years went by. On every ship there was a committee of crew members to help get the food to be better, and it did help.

On a few of the smaller ships I worked on we were somewhat lucky in that because there was so few staff members on board the small ship, they did not have a staff mess, just and officers and crew mess. So we ate in the back of the dining room having the same food as the passengers. As good as that was, there was a few drawbacks, like each meal taking about an hour to get you appetizer, soup or salad and entrée not to mention if you wanted dessert. This made it difficult to run and grab a bite and go to work, you had to plan around a long meal.

Money was another thing at dinner, we would always be ordering a bottle of wine at dinner and that adds up quickly. As far as healthy is concerned, I remember on one ship I was on in South East Asia, the dining room manager came to our table during a dinner and had us to look at a new menu he had created. He asked all of us what we thought each meal's sodium, fat and other nutritional details were and it was the consensus of all of us at the table that was put down on the menu for how healthy each meal was. No real testing or anything, we just made it up.

Now I know you are wanting some stories right now, and when I think of the dining room, I always think about when I worked on the S/S

Seabreeze for Dolphin cruise lines. I did not see this personally, but had enough versions of the story to be able to decipher what really happened.

This is the story of a honeymoon gone very bad. One night on our budget cruise ship the S/S Seabreeze of then Dolphin cruise lines, a couple who had just got married a few days earlier prior to the cruise and were having dinner in the dining room at a table with six other passengers. I was told by others at the table that dinner was going very nicely, the food was good, they were all laughing and that the honeymoon couple were chugging the wine like they were on their honeymoon, oh they were so everyone thought that was ok.

Then in an instant things changed, for no real reason that anyone at the table could remember, the newly married man did a full arm back, closed fist punch to his brides face, right between the eyes. The bride was knocked back in her chair and was on her back on the floor knocked out. By the time the unconscious bride hit the floor, the three other men at the table tackled the husband and they all went down on pinning the flailing man to the floor of the dining room.

Here is where I first knew that something had happened. I lived on the ship in an inside cabin (no windows for a year and a half, uggg) and as I was heading to go to work at the dive desk, I was going down the passenger hallway and saw one of the security guards sitting in a chair just outside one of the passenger cabins. I knew enough not to ask and went on my merry way to work. It did not take long to find out what had happened as within a few minutes of getting to the desk for work, the assistant cruise director told me what had happened in the dining room the night before. Later in the cruise I ended up speaking with most of the people who were at the dinner table in question and many at adjoining tables to get what really happened. This was a small ship of 600 passengers so little went on that you did not find out about.

What happened to the newlywed couple you might be wondering, well she was ok, but with a huge black eye. They moved her to a new cabin and put hubby on cabin arrest for the rest of the cruise. As I said earlier, this was an old ship and did not have a brig or holding cell like modern cruise ships do. Who knows what happened to their marriage, but no matter what, I'm sure it was not smooth seas.

Well I see I have strayed a little bit from my NLC diver days and thus should tell you about the time we got laid off at midnight on New Year's

Eve (Happy New Year's). Life with NCL was good and I was looking forward to another year at sea, but as I've mentioned earlier in this book, things don't always happen like you think. It was about 10:00PM outside the disco on the M/S Seaward and I was dressed in my tuxedo and getting ready to work the lounge during the New Year's celebration as I was assigned to do as part of my cruise staff duties by the cruise director. We had been busy preparing the lounge for the party when the assistant cruise director comes and tells me that he needs me and the other three divers to be in the cruise directors office at 1:00AM, and by the look on his face and the tone in his voice, I could tell the meeting was not to toast the New Year.

Up until this point I had not had anything to drink as I usually don't like drinking on New Year's because that is the night I refer to as "Amateur Night". For some it is the one night of the year they drink and go crazy and for me, that is the night I like to have all my wits about me while everyone else is losing theirs. After the assistant cruise director left the lounge, I changed my mind on not drinking, went to the bar and asked for two B-52 shots and downed them one right after the other. After that I just went back to work and put a smile on my face as we all rang in the New Year and everyone seem to be having a grand old time, except for us divers who were wondering what the hell the 1:00AM meeting was all about.

The time finally came and we four divers and the assistant cruise director joined the cruise director in his cabin. He did not beat around the bush, but just quickly said that this was one of the hardest things he had ever had to do, but he was instructed by the shore side offices to inform us that the contract with the company I worked for to do the diving operations for NCL was not renewed and that we would all be signed off the ship when we got back to Miami in four days.

I looked around the room and was proud of my fellow divers as we all had stoic faces with not much emotion as we let it sink in. The room was quit for a moment and I broke the silence by asking the diver next to me, "Do you have that phone number for Truck Master School of Trucking, I just may need that". Everyone in the cabin quietly chuckled as we decided it was time to head out and hit the disco as passengers, not crew. We stayed up till late in the morning drinking some and swapping some stories of things that had happened while working there and how much we would miss it.

Our fellow crew members (ok, not fellow as we were off the crew list as of that moment) could not believe it when we told them what had happened and the story ran around the ship like fire and everyone wanted to come and tell us how sorry they were and how they could not believe the cruise line would do that. Our dive manager got on the phone via satellite to the owner the dive company we worked for only to find out he had no idea what was going on and that they were supposed to have signed the contract already or something like that.

The snorkel tours were canceled the rest of the cruise and we went about packing and getting ready to sign off the ship and figure out what we were going to do with our lives after NCL. Two days went by and things were just about set for our exit when we got word that the cruise director and Captain wanted to see us immediately in one of the lounges. We got our formal wear on (it was formal night again) and headed up to the lounge, what could they do to us know I thought. But it was not more bad news but good news. The captain informed us our contracts were extended four months and that we were to go back to work immediately and do our tours in Cozumel that we had previously canceled.

We were all very happy to still have a job, even it was to be for a short time, at least we could plan. They started laying off divers and went to a bare staff until finally it was over, the dive company lost the contract with NCL and NCL started doing their own diving tours with their own employees and no longer contracted out those services. A few divers switched to work for NCL, but most of us did not want to work for the cruise line themselves and we headed back home or to wherever the next part of our lives would take us.

For me it was back to southern California and back to the dive shop in the harbor where I had worked for a few weeks just before getting my first job on ships. I have to say I really enjoyed being an actual Scuba instructor instead of just leading snorkeling tours. The waters off of California are still the most exciting diving I have ever done. The Caribbean and nice clear waters are nice, but can be boring after a time, but diving off of California was more exciting with the kelp forests and having to wear the full wetsuits, hood gloves and booties.

As the months went by, I found myself looking for another adventure (hey, I was still young and dumb you know). So I decided to head out and make some more luck for myself in the way of going on a dive vacation. How does going on a vacation give you luck, well I went on vacation in Grand Cayman in the Cayman Islands as that is top place I really wanted to work next. I did not want to go through another year of phone calls and sending out resume's, nope, this time I was going to just go there, dive and interview with as many dive shops as would listen to me.

With a bunch of resumes with my photo attached I headed out to Grand Cayman in August of 1992, I remember the time as I flew there two days after hurricane Andrew devastated South Florida. One of my old dive managers that lived in Miami was nice enough to pick me up at 6:00AM at the Miami International Airport to give me a tour of the devastation during my four hour layover before continuing on to Grand Cayman. It was incredible to see all the destruction and I was glad I was not there during it.

I landed in Grand Cayman and headed out to Coconut Harbor where for the next seven days I would be diving the walls of the West Side in Cayman and looking for a job, what can I say, I am a multi-tasker. The dive operation I was diving with was Parrots Landing and they were great, professional and I was able to get an interview with the manager. I still think he felt he had to give me a few minutes of his time because I spent all that money on a week of diving at Parrots Landing. The interview went well and he told of some things I would need to work in Grand Cayman like a letter from the police that I did not have a warrant for my arrest, and I would need multiple references and he explained how to work there, Parrots Landing would have to get me work visa and that took some time to get.

Even though he did not offer me a job, I felt somewhat confident that I might be able to get a job in one of the couple of hundred diver operations on the island, then fate struck and I did not look for anymore interviews on Cayman. I had called home to say hello and let my family know I was still alive and having a good time on my dive vacation. They said the man I used to work for who owned the dive company that contracted with NCL had called and wanted me to call him back. I got off the phone and called him right away to see what he was calling me about.

He answered the first time I called and said he had landed another dive contract, this time with Costa Cruise lines. Pretty much the same thing as NCL except there would be no cruise staff duties, and instead of a Bahamian private island, they had a small island off the coast of the Dominican Republic that they were developing for their passengers. The job would start in a month and he wanted to know if I wanted to come back to work for him. Of course I said yes even though there were some not so good things about the job. It was only going to pay $500 a month and then we would get commission off of our sales, hmmmmm, ok, I'll take the gamble I thought and enjoyed the rest of my dive vacation and not looking for work.

Back home I quit the dive shop (again) and got ready to head back to sea. My family was not all too thrilled that I was leaving again, but understood and was supportive to my wandering ways. It was like reunion of sorts when I signed on the M/S Costa Classica as the other three divers were friends of mine that had I worked with back at NCL.

It felt good to be back on a ship again, and this one was brand new at the time. The M/S Costa Classica was a few months old and was on its first season in the Caribbean doing Eastern and Western alternating routes meaning you sail the Eastern Caribbean one week and the Western the next week and then back to the Eastern. It was my favorite Caribbean route because since you did not do the same route every week, it kept things much fresher and non-repetitive as compared to a route that never changes.

I thought of myself as a seasoned crew member as I had done five different ships at my time with NCL, but as I was to learn, the bigger changes are cruise line to cruise line than ship to ship. With NCL, I was used to a strict following of rules and regulations, even if they did not make sense. When I signed onto the Classica, I wanted to know what rules they had so I would not unknowingly break them, but as I was to find out, it was hard to break a rule on Costa Cruise Lines as there really were no rules.

The way I summed up Costa is that I would call them "unorganized", but you have to have at least some organization to be "un" if you know what I mean. There was no curfew like we had at NCL, we had passenger cabins as they had run out of crew cabins. The whole time I was on the ship, the divers never did a life boat drill as they kind of forgot we were on board and we did not remind them that we did not attend the passenger or crew lifeboat drills. In a way it was like the startup of a company with regards to the snorkeling tours on Costa. They had never had divers on their ships before, so they did not know really what to do with us, so they just let us do our jobs which we did and we had good sales and good comments from the passengers.

One surprising thing working on a Costa Ship was the wine. The staff mess was pretty good with lots of Italian meals which is not surprise being on an Italian ship. At the end of the buffet line you could ask for wine and they would give you a half carafe of what I thought was a descent red table wine. This came in really handy when we did not have any money as the pay was really bad during this contract, so it was nice to be able to go and have a free drink or two.

I'm sure you are wanting to hear some stories from my time on the Classica, and unfortunately, the stories that come to mind on my experience there are ones of the lack of safety and downright dangerous actions taken by the officers of the Costa. When I heard about the M/S Costa Concordia hitting the rocks and capsizing in 2012, I remember that I just shrugged my shoulders and said, "That's Costa". It was no surprise to me at all, the only surprise is that it took so long for an incident like this to happen and here are some reasons why.

As I mentioned before, Costa had a small island they called "Serena Cay" which its real name was Catalina Island. It is located off the south side of the Dominican Republic near the famous golf resort of Casa de Campo. Like NCL's private island, there was no pier to dock at, so you had to take a tender to get to shore. The Classica being a new ship had four of its life boats that were both a life boat and a tender so the ship could be self-sufficient and not need shore side tenders to ferry the passengers to and from the ship to the shore.

Since the divers were the first ones to go ashore to prep for the passengers visit, we would board the ship's tender at the embarkation deck level and then be lowered down into the water where we would go straight to the small dock on the island and we could get to work setting up for the day. Pretty much every time we were lowered down in the tender, they would screw it up, and screw it up meaning that they could not lower the damn thing straight and what would end up happening is the bow and stern (back) of the tender would start taking turns banging against the ship.

One memorable time half way down the windows of the tender on the side of the ship shattered. I then took hold of my handheld VHF radio I had with me and pressed the transmit button and shouted "Our father who art in heaven, Hallowed be thy name…" and I continued it all the way down to the water. The bridge and officers heard it as did everyone else with a radio. Luckily no one was ever hurt, but our nerves were sure shattered every time we went down, but that was our job and we did it.

Another time I was on a float in the cove watching over the passengers in the water, when a tender went by near us, but still in its proper tender lane. The only issue was the tender driver was going like a bat out of hell and created a large wake which was extremely dangerous to my snorkelers that were close to the rocky shoreline in very shallow water. I made a complaint with the Staff Captain later that day when I got back on board, and within ten minutes of his getting my complaint, I was called by his secretary to his office.

As soon as I arrived in his office, he started to tell me I was mistaken and that the tender was traveling at its proper speed. I insisted that it was going too fast, which made him start to get angry and begin to raise his voice at me. Once I said, "You can call my shore side manager who was on the float with me at the time and he can confirm what I say". That is when his demeanor completely changed. His voice became very calm as he said, "Now we don't need to get shore side involved in this". Apparently shore side was watching them closely and he did not feel like this was a battle he wanted to fight. From then on, the tenders mostly followed the no wake area and that issue was over.

Yet another time the ship was at the island performing tender operations on the port (left) side of the ship which just so happened to be the windward side as well. The tenders were bouncing up and down like a Merry Go Round gone crazy, while on the starboard (right) side of the ship it was nice and calm as that side was being protected by the ship and it was like a calm lake next the ship on that side. I asked the officer in charge why we did not tender on the leeward side to which he just shouted "You don't knowaa what you areaa talking about (that was not a typo, but trying to convey his Italian accent as he yelled at me).

I found the Italians to be the worst sailors I had encountered thus far as well as being very disappointed with them in general. When I found out I would be working on an Italian ship, I thought great, they are the Amore people. Then after being on board I found them to be arrogant, back stabbing and completely not caring about the passengers.

Not too long after being on board the Classica, I started dating the fitness instructor. I had no idea that an Italian officer liked her until I was walking down the hallway and as I passed three officers, I heard something and look back. There I see two of the officers restraining the third one who was yelling at me for stealing his girlfriend.

Dating on a ship is always an interesting thing. From my experience and observations of over a decade on ships, it seems that "dating" really does not happen like it does on land. The environment is completely different as you see these people every day. It is like dating someone from your work, but then you go home at night and have you own life until you see them again at work or when you decide to spend time outside of work with them. On ships, what happens is one day you are flirting, the next day, one of you is moving into the others cabin (assuming one of you has their own cabin).

That is what happened to me on the Classica. The funny thing was her cabin was a single cabin which shared a bathroom with another cabin for two crew. So I ended up sharing a bathroom with three women and living in a cabin with my girlfriend that was about the size of a walk in closet, I mean it was hard for the two of us to walk around the cabin as there was only a few square feet of walking area. It was too small for me to keep clothes there so I just brought what I needed and was constantly walking back to my cabin which was on the other end of the ship to change. We affectingly call that journey, "The walk of shame".

There is nothing like walking back to you cabin at 7:00AM in a tuxedo as people pass you by on their way to work and give you a long look and a chuckle. All you can do is smile and get back to your cabin as soon as you could.

Life on the Classica was pretty good although the money was really bad and at least I had a job. It was still the early 1990's when the US economy was tanking and jobs were hard to come by. Then as things happened on ships, I got transferred for a month from the ship to the private island. Great you are thinking, it is just like NCL's Private

Island, paradise on earth, well not exactly. There was no place to live on the island, so me and one other diver had an apartment in the town of La Romana which was on the mainland of the Dominican Republic.

It was a two bedroom apartment on the bottom floor with amenities such as a kitchen, one bathroom, a washing machine, but no dryer, instead you had an open area that was enclosed with chain link fence to keep anyone from stealing your laundry as it hung up to dry. Another amenity was two locals with pistol grip shotguns patrolling the grounds from sunset to sunrise.

Life there was definitely different as I learned about living in a third world nation. I enjoyed my time there, but was glad to get back to the ship a month later. There were no wild stories while I was in La Romana except to say I got to go and see some local baseball games and drinking Bill Brugal rum which was $3.00 a bottle and a very good rum which I would drink today.

Getting back on the Classica after my month in the Dominican Republic was like going home in a way. I was really getting used to living at sea, working seven days a week and all kinds of hours, getting paid little for so many hours worked. My girlfriend and I were enjoying being together all the time and all in all I was very happy with life.

Then not long after getting back on the ship, my girlfriend, the fitness instructor was fired as she and the Captain did not get along at all and they had many arguments over the gym. Why would a Captain and fitness instructor have arguments over a gym, well it was mainly because the gym was right over the bridge and the officers cabins, and when the officers were taking their naps during "International Nap Time", or INT as I called which was between 2:00PM – 4:00PM, the banging noise from the gym would keep them up. My girlfriend was a New Yorker, born in Israel, grew up in England until a teenager, then moved to New York. She could speak Hebrew one moment, then with a nice polite English accent another and then say "Yo Mother FU*%er" in the next and she did have that New York attitude which did not go will with our Italian Captain.

So she is signing off the ship the next time we reach Miami and I end up with a huge decision to make about my life. If I stay on the ship, then that would obviously mean breaking up with my girlfriend, if I leave and quit the ship, then I had no idea how we would survive as I was getting paid very little and had not been able to save up much money for something like moving somewhere and setting up a life.

I will never say that I am the sharpest crayon in the box, and definitely was not at that moment as I told the owner of the company I work for that I would be following my heart and signing off the ship in Miami (ahhhhhhh). He understood and told me I had a job if I needed one (and if he had an opening of course).

The next Miami day me and my girlfriend left the ship and headed out into the big city to find what we would do. There was plenty of drama the next few days, but I don't think you are reading this book to hear stories about Miami, so I'll make it brief. We got an apartment on South Beach, I got a job at a restaurant on Ocean Drive in Miami Beach as a waiter. She got a job in a hotel running the fitness activities and life was good for a few months. We were broke, but happy and working hours like we were on a cruise ship. Eventually things got tense and we were arguing and one day I said I will go and get a job in the islands and she said to me, "You'll never get a job in the islands".

She should not have said that and as luck would have it, one phone call later I had a job in Grand Cayman. Remember that resort I went to on vacation in Grand Cayman to look for a job, but then got the job on Costa during that vacation. Well I called them up, they said yes they would love to have me and they started the work permit process. I told my girlfriend I would be gone in two weeks, we sublet the apartment, she moved back to New York and I went to live in another paradise.

My time in Grand Cayman as a dive instructor, boat captain, sailing captain was incredible. Beautiful diving along deep walls, colorful reefs and not having to wear shoes to go to work. We worked 5 ½ days a week, got paid little and the expenses were high. After spending a few weeks on one of the divers couch, I got a room in a four bedroom apartment along South Sound. It was only about fifteen minute bike ride to get to work. The days were long and I remember coming home some days after working thirteen hour of diving and sailing and filling tanks, I would fall on my bed and fall asleep still in my shorts and tank top from work and then wake up in the morning all dressed for work.

At first they told me it would be years before they would let me captain one of the dive boats, but within a month, I was driving boats and was one of the Captains of a sixty foot catamaran. I learned a lot about driving boats and sailing as well as learning the dive business from a Caribbean island point of view. My work permit was soon ending and I was in the process of getting my yearlong work permit when I got a call on Cayman again from the dive company I worked for on ships. He said he had a new contract for a brand new ship with Costa, the M/S Romantica and that he really needed me to setup the new ship and be the manager of dive operations.

I really did not want to leave Grand Cayman, I thought I could live there for the rest of my life and be very happy. But I am a sucker when someone needs me and I was talked back into coming back to Costa and running the dive operations on a cruise ship. They were not very happy at Parrots Landing when I told them I would not be staying on the island and they could stop the paperwork for my extended work permit.

Two days after I quit Parrots Landing, I was bringing in a dive boat to the dock and the manager of Parrots Landing was waiting for me. As I pulled up I said, "What, you are going to kick me off the island before I am supposed to leave in a few weeks". He said no, just the opposite and then proceeded to tell me that the owner of Parrots Landing had given him a task of making sure I stayed and they offered me the top dollar they paid anyone there and some other benefits, but I told them I was not leaving for money or because I was not happy, I was leaving because of loyalty which apparently made them want me to stay even more.

So I flew out of Cayman back to California with the help of my parents who sent me a plane ticket as I did not have much money as you do not work as a dive instructor in Cayman to be rich. I had a month in California before the new contract started on the M/S Romantica so I started doing "extra" work for movies. I got a two day gig on the movie "Threesome". Now hold on, it was not that kind of movie as the title would suggest, it was with Lara Flynn Boyle, Stephen Baldwin and Josh Charles.

It was being filmed around and on the UCLA campus and I got to stand around all day and wait. Then they picked me out of the crowd of extras to be in a night time scene outside the library, free pizza and an extra $20 so why not. I can be seen for a split second as Lara Flynn Boyle runs out of the library and right past me on the steps, my one second of fame in the movies. During the shoot I met a nice girl who was also an extra in the movie and we started going out together for a few weeks until I was going back to ships, but as I was to learn again, life does not go as planned, and my current plan was not going to pan out.

One week before I was to go back to ships, the owner of the dive company called me to inform me that he had lost the contract on the Romantica and that he did not have a job for me. Crap Crap Crap I thought, what the hell was I supposed to do now!!! I had no idea as I had little money and few options. I know you want to get back to stories on cruise ships so I'll make this brief.

I kept dating the girl I had met as an extra on the movie set, I'll call her Becky, not her real name, but that will be her name for this book. For work, I got a job at a Blank Angus restaurant in Thousand Oaks as a waiter. It was nice to be working on land again, but I missed the sea and ships and had to figure out how to get back, so it was like deja vu being back at my parents' house, getting a resume together (of course not forgetting the photo to attach to the resume) and trying to get a job on cruise ships.

This time it would not be as easy as the last one, but more like trying to get my first job on ships. It took many months, tons of phone calls and mailed resumes but this time it was a little bit different as I had a girlfriend and we did not want to break up so I was looking for a job for both of us on ships. I trained her as a scuba diver, and then got her all the way up to certified Dive Master in no time and I landed us a job as a "couple" dive team for a dive company called Aqua Fun Adventures. It was very similar to the other dive company I worked for on NCL and Costa, but this company had contracts with Dolphin Cruise line and their sister line Majesty Cruise Line and no private island.

It was challenging to get a job as a couple, especially with no interview besides phone interviews. After a lot of work in training Becky as a diver and getting us an actual job on ships, her and I were off to sea, the first time for her, the third time for me. Now Dolphin Cruise Line was not as nice as NCL or Costa. I referred to them as a "budget" cruise line or as I later came to call them, "trailer park trash" cruise lines. That may seem mean but it was funny at the time. Actually the line had some great passengers in that they really loved cruising and the line was known for one thing, and that was their food. By far they had the best food I have ever had on ships for passengers or crew.

We had a staff mess on the Seabreeze, but we ordered our meals off the passenger menu, so the next few years I ate very well, although it was the same food every week, I know I know, stop complaining. By the way, one very surprising item was pineapple chunks covered with horseradish, I know it sounds crazy but those two items combined was incredible. The sweetness of the pineapple mellowed the heat of the horseradish; give it a try some time.

One Miami day on the Seabreeze, one of the staff received ten boxes of good'ol Kraft Macaroni and cheese and we asked the chef to cook it up for us so we could have the taste of home in a way as what American kid does not grow up having Kraft Mac & Cheese. We were extremely excited when we got to the staff mess to have our taste of home. We noticed something did not look right with the Mac & Cheese and we asked the chef why it looked like that (not so much the deep orange color we knew and loved). The French chef proudly tells us that he added Gouda cheese and some other items to make it better. Obviously he did not get the fact that we wanted the taste that we grew up with. So that meal was scrapped, but his heart was in the right place so we could not get mad at him.

At the time I am writing this book, the Carnival Triumph had an engine fire in the Gulf of Mexico and it took five days for the ship to be towed to Mobile Alabama which during the five days there was no toilets, limited food and the passengers were living on the outer decks in less than ideal conditions. This reminded me of a time on the Seabreeze when the boiler "blew up" around dinner time on our way back to Miami from a cruise to the Eastern Caribbean. We did not hear a boom per say, but all of sudden the power went out just as I was getting my tux on to go to dinner and then to work at the dive desk. Soon it was obvious we were not getting any power back on that evening which meant no work and that the normality that we knew was out the window.

So Becky and I and the staff got changed into comfortable, breathable clothes as there was no air conditioning in the ship and it was hot and humid everywhere. We brought along with us a bottle of Scotch and went up to the lounge where the comedian was putting on an impromptu show in a lounge lit by flashlights and one of the staff was using a battery operated search light they got from one of the life boats as a spotlight for the show.

The highlight of the night was that there was a "meditation" group on board who believed in crystals and the power of healing through holding hands together, well you get the idea. They also believed in being able to see the future through their meditation. The comic then made fun of them saying, "Didn't they see this coming".

Becky and I went to sleep that night in our stuffy, hot & humid cabin while others decided to sleep out on deck and some who had port holes were able to get them open and let some fresh air in. All that sounded like a good idea at the time, but around 6:00AM they were able to start up the boiler (the Seabreeze was an old ship built in 1958 and was propelled through the water by steam powered turbines), when they started the boiler a thick cloud of black dust came out of the stack and since it was a nice calm windless morning, the black dust fell right back onto the deck and covered the ship.

The people sleeping on the outside decks were awaken to the feeling of being covered in ash and looked like a bunch of Al Jolson look a likes (Google Al Jolson to see what I am talking about if you don't know). Those who were "lucky" enough to get their port hole open for some fresh air in the night awoke to their cabin being covered with the black dust in every square inch nook and cranny of their cabin which took some time to clean as you can imagine.

The ship survived the night without power, toilets, air conditioning and other amenities we take for granted, but we would be six hours late getting into Miami which meant that the Lesbian cruise would be boarding late.

Did I just write Lesbian cruise, yes I did. The next cruise was a charter from a Lesbian group and the entire ship would be full of women for the next cruise which was very interesting and quite different than the gay cruise I would work on years later (that story is coming up). The ladies finally boarded the ship later in the day and we were just starting to move away from the dock to begin our ladies only cruise when the organizers started their

Lesbian conga line around the pool and outside decks.

The assistant cruise director who was my best friend on the ship watched with me as our girlfriends joined the ladies in their dance as we watched seven hundred or so woman with their hands on the hips of the woman in front of them shake and shimmy around the ship. I looked to my friend and said, "Toto, we are not in Kansas anymore" and thus started an interesting cruise like I had never encountered before. As we were sailing out of the port a small boat came by and two women in the boat took off their tops and flashed their bare breasts to the screaming woman on the decks as it raced passed the Seabreeze. In all my years of sailing I had not, and never again saw women flashing their breasts during sail away and I had to think it was more than a coincidence that we were on a Lesbian cruise and woman were flashing their breasts at the ship, you decide.

All in all the cruise was very good cruise, the ladies were very nice and not too wild, but one thing I do remember that stood out during the cruise was the female comedians they had brought with them for some evening entertainment. Now I grew up with Eddie Murphy, Andrew Dice Clay and other "raunchy" comedians, but I had never blushed or felt like a stranger in a strange land like I did during those comedic shows. The content of their act was very sexually explicit and since it was their charter, the comics were allowed to use pretty much any words they wanted to which they did to describe female sexual acts and things to know like how to turn a women into a Lesbian.

One great item of the Lesbian cruise was the fact that Becky and I sold out of our snorkeling tours and rental gear the first night of the cruise, so if the weather cooperated, it was going to be a very good money week for us as we were paid 100% commission. If the tour(s) were canceled for any reason, we did not get any money and we had some cruises where our income was zero. The weather was nice to us and we had a banner week and had a great time taking the ladies snorkeling and watching them sensually cover each other with sun tan lotion (come on, who could blame me).

Compared to the Atlantis Gay cruise I was to be on years later, the Lesbians were a quiet group but they had a great time, we had good comments and I believe they charted the ship again a few years later.

That year we had another charter that was for deaf people. We thought it was great that people with the loss of hearing could have an entire cruise for them, with entertainment and comedians and everything using sign language, but it presented challenges for us who were not used to not using voice as a means of communication.

The charter brought on a few people on the cruise before to train and prep the crew for the deaf charter. I remember being in the disco during the day and having a meeting with those representatives where they "taught" us how to communicate with the deaf. I was very impressed on how much they stressed to just treat them "normal" as the passengers would work with us to communicate what they needed. The training took a strange turn when they started teach the staff how to "pick up" the deaf passenger that were boarding on the next cruise. They taught us how to ask their name and other simple questions including, "Do you want to go back to my cabin with me".

Yes, they actually were teaching us how to take a deaf passenger back to their or your cabin to have sex. As I stated they wanted us to treat them "normally", and I could not argue with that logic. For me it was an interesting cruise taking deaf people snorkeling and doing all our normal verbal communications via someone doing sign language to translate what we were saying and helping answer their questions. I watched some of the crew "hook up" with some of the passengers and found it odd to be on a cruise where the ship stated it was ok to sleep with a passenger. For all of my cruises, this would be the only one where they openly condoned it. This did not apply to me as I had my girlfriend on board that I worked with so we were just spectators in the flurry of hand signs and people trying to get together using a means other than talking, but then again, when two people want to have sex, they will find a way to communicate.

Those cruises have fond memories for me and I am glad I was able to be on them to experience the differences people have in their lives, either being a Lesbian, or being deaf. It is important to remember that there is no "normal", and that the way you live your life is not how everyone lives theirs and that there really is no right or wrong, just different and it is good to experience those differences to help better understand the world we live in together.

Not all cruises had such fond memories and this story involves one of the greatest life lessons I have learned to which I still think of today in my daily life. It involved the Captain of the Seabreeze and happened during one of our weekly managers meeting where all the ship's managers would meet with the Captain to go over the business of the ship and address any issues just as you would in any business.

The Captain asked me about a complaint from a passenger where he accused Becky and myself of being rude to him which is something taken very seriously by the ship. The incident involved a male guest who was walking around the snorkel boat with fins on. Now walking around with fins on is dangerous and even more so on a small moving boat and we had to be strong in having him take off his fins when not in the water and for the life of me, I have no idea why the man wanted to walk around a boat with fins on. We were not rude, but we did not let him have his way either which passengers do not like.

I informed the Captain of what happened to which we kept telling me I was wrong and not to do that again. Now when it comes to safety, I do not back down from anyone and this Captain was "pushing my buttons". He kept on prodding me until I had had enough and I remember saying loudly across the room that Becky and I were the only ones on the ship that maintained a one million dollar liability policy for our job and that no one, including a Captain would make me do something to incur liability and so on. While I was loudly stating this and pointing my finger at the Captain, he was shouting and pointing at me until finally he just shook his hands in the air and told me to be quiet in his heavy Greek accent.

After leaving the meeting I thought, well this is it and went back to tell Becky that we would probably be getting fired and signing off the ship when we get back to Miami. We did not get fired and here is why. The Captain really did not care about the incident, as I said he was Greek and they are very manly and a people of standing up for what you believe. The Captain had been testing me to see if I was a man and if I would stand up for myself and apparently I passed his Greek manly test and he never questioned my work again, although we did have a few tense moments again while we were working together which I will tell you now.

We were in Grand Cayman one day on the S/S Seabreeze and the seas were not very good off the island. They were five feet or so with white caps blowing and not very nice for a tender ride to the island or back to the ship. It was really crazy as we took the first tender ashore and got tossed around like a cork in violent seas. The kicker was that the ship was over a mile off the island where the seas were rough, while the waters closer to the island where the other ships were anchored, was nice and calm.

Some of the passengers on my tender ashore were crying and praying and they were scared for their lives. Was it that bad, not to someone was used to boats and life on the ocean, but someone not used to being in a small boat in rough seas, it was terrifying. When I got to shore, I comforted the passenger the best I could and got them on their way to enjoy the island and hopefully not fear the ride back to the ship.

I decided not to go on our snorkel trip and sent Becky to run it without me as I felt I was needed on the pier more than on our tour which did not have that many people on and Becky could handle it easily on her own that day. So I stayed on the pier to help assure our passengers they were ok when they got to shore from their terrifying tender ride to the island. It was getting ridiculous as I watched the other ships that were closer to shore run normal tender operation and their passengers were happy vs. our scarred to death ones.

Enough was enough so I grabbed my VHF radio and contacted the Seabreeze's bridge and told them I wanted to speak with the Captain. This was not a normal request at all, and they fought me on it until they gave in and called the Captain to the bridge (I think he was taking his nap at the time). He immediately yelled at me for contacting him to which I returned the favor and spoke very loudly how he was scarring our passenger to the point of tears and fearing for their lives and that I wanted him to bring the ship in closer for safer tender operations. Now a lowly diver does not tell a Captain of a ship how to sail his ship or conduct tender operations and thus my request did not go over that well as a volley of shouting went back and forth from our radios.

In the end he told me he would speak to me later about this and left the bridge leaving me pissed off and mad on the pier. Of course I had this conversion with the Captain out of earshot of the passengers as that would not be profession, although I was not sure how professional I was being and anyone listening on the VHF on that channel could hear our "conversation". It was a miracle, but the ship actually did come closer to the island and the tender ride was becoming more normal with just a little bit of bouncy seas between the ship and the shore.

The rest of the day went better although knowing I would have a big confrontation with the Captain made me stress out and spent my time thinking how our "conversation" would go later that day. Well the day finally ended and we were back on the Seabreeze after a nice and quick tender ride to the ship. I got a call from the bridge that the Captain wanted to see me at the Captain's cocktail party which was starting soon. Here we go I was thinking and wondering how the evening would turn out, would I be fired? Would he call my dive company and ask for me to be removed from his ship (which has happened to other dive couples on this cruise line).

I got my tuxedo on and Becky and I went to the main lounge to see the Captain. My shoulders were up and back straight as I entered the lounge and preparing for the argument that was coming. The Captain saw me and walked straight over to me, here it goes, let the battle begin I thought to myself. He confidently walked up to me and held his hand out to shake mine, which I did, and then he leaned over and said, "Thank you for all your help today, I know it was a tough day". What the hell I thought, was he joking, but apparently he was not. He told me to go over to his table and we would have a drink.

I found out later that people had been telling the Captain how rough the ride was and how nice the diver Guy was on the pier and so on. We had a few drinks with the Captain and we were all best friends which was not how I imagined the night would be going, but the Captain knew I was a man of conviction and stood up when the time came and he respected that. If I would have done that with a Norwegian or Italian Captain, I would have probably been thrown overboard or keel hauled.

The lesson learned from these confrontations is you need to react differently to different people or different nationalities in this case. This lesson served me well in Asia and other parts of the world where we do not always think the same and we still need to work together.

Not all of my dealing with this Captain was confrontational; I actually thought he was a good Captain and a nice man. One day on the Seabreeze we were in Jamaica and I was on phone to Grand Cayman where the ship was scheduled to be the next day and telling them what my tour numbers were as I normally did. My Cayman operators told me the seas on the West side were bad and the ships had gone that day to the anchoring backup area of the South Sound. Later in the day I saw the Captain on the dock and told him what the ships did that day in Cayman and that there would be a good chance we would have to go to the South Sound to anchor the next day, or blow out of the island and not stop there. He asked me what this South Sound was and that he had never been there to which I let me know about the area, the entrance to the reef and that I lived in South Sound when I lived on Grand Cayman and used to anchor our dive boats there when the weather was bad on the West side.

He thanked me and that was that. Then the next morning I got a call in the hallway, let me stop here and let you know how old the ship was. In certain areas of the ship, crew cabins did not have phones, instead you had a phone in your hallway that you would use to communicate with others on the ship, besides the Norway, it was the only ship I worked on like that. So the hallway phone rings, someone in the hall answered it and knocked on my cabin to say the call was for me. I went to the phone where a stern Greek voice said, "Come to the bridge immediately".

Great, here we go again I thought and raced up to the bridge as fast as I could. I was breathing heavily as I knocked on the door to the bridge and breathed deeply to regain my normal breathing back. The door opened and I was told the Captain wanted to see me. As I approached the Captain, I looked out and saw the familiar view of the South Sound of Grand Cayman. I looked to the West and could almost see where I used to live during my time living in Grand Cayman.

The Captain then asked me how to get in the opening of the reef to anchor in the sound. What the hell I thought, he is asking me? I'm just a lowly diver, not a port pilot. I guess I should say what a port pilot is, they are Captains who work with a port and are the experts on every square inch of that port and they usually come on board when coming near a port, or when leaving a port and they are in charge of the ship's navigation during this time. Grand Cayman did not have port pilots as they usually just anchored off the West Side as there is no port in Grand Cayman big enough for a cruise ship to dock.

So there I was with the bow pointing toward Grand Cayman's South Side and everyone on the bridge looking at me to give them direction. Now I am not going to kid you, part of me wanted to just leave the bridge and get out of there, but that is not what you do on ships. They ask you to do something and you do it to the best of your ability. Looking back on that day, I should have told the Captain I was not qualified to guide the ship between the reef and into the anchoring area and let him make a decision on how to get in, or just not stop and have a sea day which would not go over well with the paying passengers.

It was one of those "man up" moments in my life and with the most confidence I could muster in me, I walked up near the front of the bridge. I scanned the area to get a fix on where exactly we were in relation to the opening in the reef. After looking and trying to remember the reefs layout, I saw what I was looking for. "Rudders 15 degrees to port, ahead slow" I said with a commanding voice to the helmsman. If only they had known I could not feel my legs at that moment and I was wishing to be wearing an adult diaper for the first time in my life.

"Rudders mid ship" I said as the opening to the reef was at the bow of the ship and we slowly entered the South Sound. "Rudders 20 degrees to starboard" I said as the ship then turn slowly to starboard to the middle of the anchoring area of the sound. "Anchor to the waterline" I said as I was like a parrot repeating the works and phrases I had heard on the times I was on the bridge during maneuvers like this. I was waiting for the Captain to jump in and contradict me at any time, but I glanced over to him to see him watching where his ship was and what it was doing very closely, but he looked calm and cool, which was the opposite to how I was feeling at the time.

"Rudders Mid Ship, all engines stop" I said as the ship crept to what I remembered as the best anchoring for a ship that size in the sound. I did not say to drop the anchor as that was something I believed the Captain should do. As the ship came to a near stop right where I wanted it, I looked at the Captain and told him this was where he should anchor and then pointed out some areas of the reef to be cautious of and then he looked at me and said, "Now go do your tours" in his heavy Greek accent.

I don't know how, but my legs did actually work and I left the bridge thinking that I was just stepping out of an episode of the Twilight Zone and asking myself if I really did just guide a cruise ship to its anchorage through a reef. Getting back to my cabin I told Becky what had just happened and she could not believe as I still could not.

Luckily the Captain did not ask me back to the bridge later when we were leaving and even more lucky that he never asked me to the bridge to guide the ship again. I was proud of what I had done, thankful I did crash the ship and knew I never wanted to do that again and luckily, I never had to.

It seemed like Grand Cayman was a magnet for me and for incidents that never seemed to happen in any other ports. One day while in Grand Cayman, I was in a lounge getting my passengers ready for their snorkeling trip when I was told by the cruise staff that the tour was canceled. "Who canceled it" I asked as the only people to cancel one of my tours were the tour operator or myself. I was informed that the cruise director canceled it. Quickly I went to the gangway where the cruise director should be and found her to ask why she was canceling the tour. She said the seas looked a little too rough for snorkeling and she assumed I would want to cancel. Now to assume just makes an ass out of you and I felt like saying that, but did not. Instead I told her the area we were conducting the snorkeling was nice and calm as my tour operator had told me earlier that morning of the conditions at the snorkel site.

Here is where things went sideways so to speak as by this time, it was too late to do the snorkel tour and be able to run the one scheduled for the afternoon and thus really had to be canceled now. I was not a happy camper as this was affecting my income, no tour, no pay for Becky and Guy and the passengers missed out on their chance to snorkel in Grand Cayman. The day went on and we ran the afternoon tour with no problems and had good conditions at the snorkeling site.

That night I wrote my report of the days activities which goes to the Cruise Director, Chief Purser and then to the Captain with their reports and I included a part in the report that from now on I would like only the dive manager to cancel a snorkeling tour as we were the ones in contact with the tour operator and know whether or not a tour should actually be canceled.

Fine I thought, at least that shouldn't happen again, but a can of worms was being opened that would turn into drama for the next few days. I received the copy of my report back with comments from the Cruise Director as I usually did, but something was wrong. My whole part in the report about the Cruise Director canceling my tour and asking that only the dive manager be able to cancel them in the future was taken out. What the hell I thought, and went to ask the Cruise Director what was going on. She sat Becky and I in her cabin and said told us we were wrong and she was the Cruise Director and I was to never write anything about her losing revenue in a report again.

There was not much I could do but sit there and listen to her crap and try my best to explain the logic of the situation, but my logic was falling on deaf ears. I was pretty pissed off when we left her cabin and I had to think about what I was going to do. I'll spare you the details, but basically I went and told the Staff Captain about what had happened. He was a nice Greek man that the crew affectively called "Bulldog" and he liked that name.

Now I am not a tattle tale or a snitch, but I also don't like anyone changing my reports and handing them off as if I wrote it and I had to do something about it. I talked with Bulldog about it and I told him I was a man, and I don't want anyone misrepresenting me and that I will stick by what I write in my report as a man should (remember the Greek like the manly stuff), he said he would look into it and get back with me. Well you know what hit the fan at that point. Becky and I got called into the Chief Purses office with the Cruise Director and got yelled out for going behind their backs. I rightfully informed that it was wrong to pass off my edited report to the Captain as mine and the volleys went back and for until we finally left and everyone involved was pissed off.

Once again we were wondering if we would be kicked off the ship, but that was not to happen.

We eventually got called back to the Staff Captain's office where he told us "officially" we were wrong, but then said that in his and the Captain's eyes, we were right. Then he went on to tell me that the reason this issue became such a big stink is because it brought to light that the Chief Purser and the Cruise Director were editing all the managers reports so they would look good no matter what, and then passed them on to the Captain as unedited reports which once the Captain found this out, he was not a happy camper to say the least.

The Chief Purser and Cruise Director got yelled at big time by the Captain and from then on, I was to send my reports directly to the Captain as well as the Cruise Director so he could be sure no "editing" of the reports could be done. Needless to say, life on board the Seabreeze had much more political drama than I had before on other ships, but then again I spent a year and a half on that ship which is a long time (I had a vacation in between my contracts on the Seabreeze and worked for on Dolphin's sister cruise line Majesty on the Royal Majesty which I will get to in a bit).

As I just mentioned, we got to go on vacation after nine months on the Seabreeze and where else would I want to go but.......Grand Cayman. Our main tour operator in Cayman also owned an all-inclusive resort there and I had asked the owner if we could come and stay for a week. I was not sure how he would take the request, but his employees had told us to ask, so we did. He told us that he would be happy to have us and so we had a great week with all expenses paid except for our airfare from Miami. I figured it would be stupid not to take advantage of some of the perks of working with shore operators. It would not be the last time that perks like this was used during my time on ships.

After our Cayman vacation and a few weeks in California to visit family and friends it was off to the Royal Majesty out of Boston and going to Bermuda, but before I go there, let me say that when we went home and talked with my family about the nine months we had been gone, it was nice to have Becky there to confirm everything we told them (not that they did not believe me), but as Becky told my family, all the stories are true and it was nice to have that confirmation so no one thought I was exaggerating the events of our time on the Seabreeze.

Off to Boston we went to board the new ship, the Royal Majesty. It was a beautiful ship that was only a year old and had just repositioned from three and four day cruises in the Bahamas, to operating out of Boston and going to Bermuda where it docked at St. George's Warf for two days, then over to downtown Hamilton for two days before heading back to Boston. It was nice to be going somewhere different and having different challenges, and boy did Bermuda have its challenges to operate snorkeling tours which I will get to.

It was not long before the stories started piling up on this ship. On one of our cruises to Bermuda, the ship seemed to hit something as we all felt like the ship "stall" for a moment a few hours after leaving Boston but everything seemed fine and the ship continued on to Bermuda. After a day at sea the following morning we were approaching St. Georges cut to get into the Warf when all of a sudden the ship made a quick turn and the harbor pilot radioed the ship to say we had a dead whale stuck on our bulbous bow (or DPR shall I say), ah, so that is what we hit when leaving Boston.

The local newspapers in Bermuda were all over the story about how a cruise ship killed a rare species of whale. They brought in maritime animal experts to dissect the carcass that ended up washing up on a beach after it was dislodge from the bow by the ships movement. Of course the whale must have been dead or almost dead to not hear a cruise ship and get out of its way.

This reminds me of when I would eventually work in Alaska (that is coming up later) and they would announce over the ship public address system "Whales off the port side" when they spotted whales. I wanted to add to the announcement, "Whales off the port side, harpoon crew man your stations". It would have been interesting how fast the rumors would have flown around the ship that it had actually harpooned some whales.

As I have said before in this book, just like on land, life is not always fair and this is a story about life not being fair for one of the crew. It was about midnight in the crew bar on the Royal Majesty and we were docked in Bermuda. A few of us were having a nice cocktail and some good conversion when a very very drunk Greek officer stumbled into the crew bar. He tried to get me angry by saying some mean things about Americans, but I did not take the bait and just waved my hand at him and ignored him.

The sound and light technician who was American and sitting with us, stood up and told the drunk officer he should leave and pointed to the door. That is when the Greek officer punched the sound and light technician in the face and he went down to the floor. The guys in the bar grabbed the Greek officer and held him away from the sound and light technician and boy did he put up a struggle, but there was about six of us on him holding him back so he could not do much to anyone.

After a minute or two, the Greek officer calmed down and then left the bar. We helped the sound and light technician up, he took the punch as well as someone could and was bleeding abit and was already getting black and blue. Now fighting on ships is grounds for immediate dismissal meaning you are signed off the ship at the next port and fired. We kind of laughed it up some and wondered what was going to happened to the officer as usually officers take care of their own if you know what I mean.

The next day I could not believe it when I heard that they had fired the sound and light technician! What the hell I thought and went straight to the Staff Captain whom I knew pretty well and he seemed like a good guy. I told him I was right there and saw everything and that the Greek officer had sucker punched the sound and light technician. He told me it was none of my business and to drop it, I kept asking why they fired him until he told me to shut up to which I looked at him straight in the eye and told him I no longer had any respect for Greek officers. He just pushed me aside and went on his way and that was that. It was a good lesson on how life is not fair. I hope there was some information I did not know about to why they fired him, but that information never surfaced and things never stay a secret on ships, so I have to assume there was none and that they were just taking care of their own.

Running snorkeling tours in Bermuda turned out to be much more challenging than in the Caribbean and the Bahamas. The tours we sold included our snorkeling gear on board that we would hand out to the passengers prior to the tour just as I had done on the all the cruise lines and ships I had worked on thus far. Becky and I would lead the tour and conduct the snorkel tour in the water and show people all the fish and coral and do our best to entertain them in the water like I had done with hundreds of snorkeling tours in the past.

Now in Bermuda, they did not like that as they wanted the ship to just use one of the local dive shops to run the tour and keep all the money in Bermuda. In order not to break the law, we worked with a local dive shop and always had a few of their instructors or dive masters with us on the beach, the snorkel boat and in the water. We did not need them, but we paid them to be there to be allowed to run the tours, just another cost of doing business. More than once I caught some locals in the bushes filming us with a camcorder to try and catch us not using local divers and breaking the law, of course we always used local divers so all they were filming was us doing our jobs and following the local Bermudian laws.

Some of the local dive shops we did not work with filed complaints against our company and Becky and me and within a month of working in Bermuda on the Royal Majesty, I found myself being summoned to the Customs house in Hamilton for an investigation into our snorkeling program. There I sat with a dozen "officials" from the Bermudian government trying to tell me I was breaking their laws and that we would be fined and our snorkeling equipment confiscated. During that first meeting I was able to assure them that we did follow the laws and had brought witnesses from the local dive shop that we worked with to confirm that we did use local divers on all of our tours.

They told me to come back the next week when we were in port for another hearing. I called the owner of the dive operation I worked for and told him he needed to sort out this customs and immigration thing in Bermuda. He told me that I had to deal with it since I was there and not to jeopardize his business or contract with the Royal Majesty. Great I thought, another thing I would never had imagined myself doing, negotiating business rights with a foreign countries custom and immigration.

The main accusation was that we were the only ones operating on Bermuda that used our own gear from our ship. For weeks we had these "hearings" and each week I was able to stall for another week. I even took photos of the NCL divers in Bermuda that were conducting their tours just like we were, but for some reason it ok for NCL to do it. They just looked at my photos and shrugged their shoulders and told me I was breaking their laws.

I guess this experience was a good one in dealing with a government. Basically nothing got done, they never stopped me from operating in Bermuda, although I had to spend a day every week in their "hearings", but in the end it was successful in that Becky and I were able to operate the tours and make some money for our company, the cruise line and a few bucks for us.

By the way, for those of you interested in taking a cruise to Bermuda, I highly suggest it. It is a beautiful place, lots of history, great beaches, nice people (excluding the customs officials) and good food. The one thing about Bermuda is it is expensive, and I mean expensive, so don't expect the sleazy street vendors and cheap trinkets like you find in the Caribbean. And what I said about not buying drugs, Bermuda is a HUGE no no. They have an incredibly strict anti-drug laws and there are more than a few crew members who are doing life in a Bermudian jail for being stupid enough to try and deal with drugs in their country.

Cruise ship tip reminder: Don't mess with drugs on cruise ships or ports.

One time while in St. George's in Bermuda, the ship had gotten some rope wrapped around one of its propellers and rudders. The Staff Captain asked me to dive under the ship, but at first I refused. He was somewhat shocked that I refused and wanted to know why. In the most polite way I could explain, I told him that I did not trust the ship while diving under it.

Meaning that although I thought the Greek's were ok sailors, better than the Italians, but nowhere near as good as the Norwegians, I did not really trust them to not start up the ships propeller for a test, or something else while I would be working under the ships stern. It turned into an argument as he really needed the rope removed and none of his officers could do it except for me. Eventually we came to an agreement, I first inspected the bridge to confirm that all the officers and bridge crew knew that there would be a diver under the ship (me), and I personally inspected that the safety flags were placed on all the controls on the ship that said "Divers Working" (or something like that, can't remember the exact phrase now).

Once I was certain that all the precautions on the bridge were taken, I then made the Captain, Staff Captain and Chief Engineer stand on the pier while I went under the ship as those were the only three people on board who could officially "start" the engines. They were not thrilled with my lack of faith in their officers, but it was my life and that is how I felt. So I went under the ship's stern and spent about an hour cutting and removing the rope that was wrapped around parts of the starboard propeller and around the starboard rudder. It appeared to be from a lobster trap was my best guess and that would mean we got it as we left the port of Boston which I explained to the Captain after I finished my dive. And for my efforts, I got paid nothing, barely a thank you from any of the senior officers. Oh well, at least I help keep the ship safe in some small way.

There are some days that live in your memory forever and this is on such memory. Most days working on cruise ships are challenging in one way or another, and then just like in life no matter where you live or what you do for a living, bad days happen. It was on a beautiful summer's day in Bermuda and the Royal Majesty was docked in St. George's. Becky and I were running snorkeling tours over to a cove on the other side of Bermuda. It was beach snorkeling and we had two different departures that morning. I sent Becky out with the first group along with our local dive masters and I stayed on the ship to organize our second group going to the cove.

I was in the lounge mid ship and looking over the beautiful port of St. George's when my cell phone rang (it was one of those huge cell phones the size of a brick with the big fixed antenna) and it was the dive master at our beach snorkeling site. He informed me that there was a medical emergency with one of our passengers. I asked if he had called for an ambulance and he stated that he had, but it would be coming from Hamilton and was not sure how long it would take to get there. I asked where Becky was and he stated he she was giving CPR to the victim.

As I began running to the gangway, I placed a call with our tour operator that handled our ground transportation and told them I needed to get to the beach snorkeling site as soon as possible due to a medical emergency there. By the time I got off the gangway and onto the pier and through the terminal building I heard a taxi van screeching around a corner heading for the terminal. At least they took my request seriously I thought to myself. The van braked just before me and I opened the door, slammed it and before I could say anything we were off like a flash to the beach site.

It was definitely a record in getting to the beach site and as we drove up to the parking area next to the cove, I flew out the door just as the taxi skidded to a halt. I was running to the cove and as I entered the area and could finally see the beach and water, I noticed about 50 people on the left area of the beach and they seemed to be talking to each other and looking toward the right area of the beach. I found our local agent who pointed me toward the right area of the cove about half way to the ocean. I looked and saw a small group of people huddled at the water's edge. I sprinted there to find the group in a few inches of water with some scatter rocks around and man lying on his back in the water and Becky doing chest compressions and some person I did not know doing mouth to mouth on the victim. As I approached I asked for a report on what happened. One of the passengers said Becky had found the snorkeler floating face down in the water and not moving and she yelled for help and the dive master on the beach met her in the shallow water where Becky had flipped the man over and dragged him to the shallow water.

It had been about 15 minutes they said since the victim was discovered and I asked who needed to be replaced in the CPR, Becky and the other person said they could use a break and some person whom I cannot remember replaced Becky doing the chest compressions and I went to replace the person who was doing the mouth to mouth.

As I look back on things, there was something ironic about what I was about to do. For years now I had carried with me a CPR mask, one that would seal around the victim's face and you would blow air into a tube to avoid direct mouth to mouth with the person, and if necessary, you could give mouth to mouth in the water where the mask would help prevent water from getting in the victim mouth.

As usual, I had my pocket mask on a belt around my waist, but in this moment, I just went and started doing mouth to mouth without the mask. As I write this, the sounds, the smells the whole scene is like I was back there. The back and forth of the inch or so of water under the victim, the smell of vomit, the stubble of the man's mustache and beard (he was on vacation, so I guess he did not shave that day or days on the cruise). I checked to make sure his airway was open by titling his head back, closed his nostrils shut with my fingers and blew to two puffs of air into the victim and as I finished the second breath, I looked at his chest to see it falling somewhat, and I knew his airway was indeed open and my breaths were making their way into the man's lungs which gave me a glimmer of hope.

He involuntarily vomited a few times and I used the water to quickly wash it away from his mouth and kept on doing the mouth to mouth. It seemed like an eternity when I finally took a moment to ask when the ambulance would be here. The dive master said they would have to come all the way from Hamilton and it would take them 30 minutes or so. Any hope I had was gone right there and then as I knew this man had a serious heart event and that without advanced life support and a hospital, there was little chance for him.

Not much could be done but to continue what I was doing and wait for the paramedics to arrive. The person doing chest compressions switched off with another person a few times, but I did not want to make anyone do the unsettling task of mouth to mouth so I just kept doing it. I felt numb as I had been on my knees in the rocky water and bending over for about 30 minutes doing breaths when out of the corner of my eye I saw the paramedics coming to the scene.

Finally I thought. I noticed they were not running or coming to us with anything more than slightly faster pace than walking. As they approached us, they were given an update as to what happened and when the dive master finished the quick synopsis of the events leading up to that moment, I saw the paramedics look at each other and give a little shrug with their shoulders. They came over to me and put a mask over the man's face and replaced me with the mouth to mouth (theirs was mask to mouth). I stood up and felt my body ache, I reached down and washed my mouth out with salt water and watched as they picked him up and put him on a stretcher and carried him to their ambulance for the 30 minute drive back to Hamilton.

It was no use I knew, the man had no sign of life besides some involuntary vomiting and there was little to no hope for him. As I walked back to the beach and the entrance of the cove, there I saw our shore side operator with her arms around a woman who was obviously the victim's wife. She was slightly crying as she watched them load her husband in the ambulance and she got on board with them for the trip to the hospital.

I was exhausted, both physically and mentally as I found Becky and gave her a hug. She had been crying as well as was many other passengers on the snorkeling trip. By this time there were only a few passengers on the beach, as many had already gone back to the ship as the good time mood of snorkeling on a tropical island had long vanished. We packed up our things and got on the last taxi van back to the pier.

The police had been on the scene at the beach and had told us we would be needed at the St.

George's police station to make a statement. I said I had to report to the ship and inform them of what had happened to which the police man said that would be fine. So we dropped off Becky and the dive master at the police station and I was dropped off at the terminal where the Royal Majesty was.

I was loaded with gear and got through the security check point and was heading to the gangway. On my way I found the Staff Captain, Chief Engineer and some other Greek officer whom I cannot remember who he was now standing on the pier. I walked up to them and asked if the Captain was on board and that I needed to speak with him. The Greek officer whose position I cannot remember said, "You don't need the Captain, the Staff Captain is right here" and then he said something else that in my current condition really pissed me off. I spoke loudly as I said to the group of officers, "I need to speak to the FU&%ing CAPTAIN". By the time I finished my outburst, the Staff Captain had taken me by the arm and pulled me away from the other officers and asked what the problem was.

I told him we had a death on our tour and I needed to update the Captain of what has happened and then I need to go to the police station to make a statement. He told me to drop off my gear and go to the Captains office. At the time, I was in no mood to ask questions or anything, so I continued to head to the gangway and I saw out the corner of my eye the Staff Captain talking on his UHF radio in Greek. After dropping off my gear, I headed to the Captains office, I knocked and then entered through the curtain (it was common on ships to leave your cabin door open and the curtain in front of your door closed).

The Captain greeted me and asked me to sit. Looking back on it now, he and the Staff Captain were extremely supportive and compassionate about the situation. As quickly and accurately as I could, I gave the Captain a report about what had happened at the beach that morning. He sat there and listened to my melancholy voice until I was done and then asked how I and Becky were doing. We had not been able to process things yet I told him. We had a boat snorkel scheduled for that afternoon and it was sold out. The Captain told me that if I wanted to cancel it, and all the water sports tours for the rest of the cruise that it would be fine with him and that Becky and I could take the rest of the cruise to recover from the ordeal.

That was unexpected as usually it is money first as with any business. I thanked him for the offer, but said that since I did not know how long we would be at the police station, that I would cancel the afternoon boat snorkel, but reschedule it for the next day as we had two days in St. George's and this was the first day there. At that time, I was not sure what we would do for the tours for the rest of the cruise, but that I would let him know by that evening as to my plans.

He shook my hand and thanked me (for what, I am really not sure) and I headed back off the ship and walked to the police station which was only about 10 minutes away. They escorted me to a room where I saw Becky and our dive master talking with an officer. I introduced myself and they said they were just about finished. The officer read back to me what he had written down about the accident and I added a few things and within about 15 minutes, we walked silently out of the police station and back to the ship.

We went to the mess for some lunch, although we did not feel like eating, but I knew we had to eat something before we went back to work to re-arrange the tours for the next few days. We had a quick bite, but did not taste any of the food. I told Becky to go back to the cabin and rest and I would take care of things.

It was time to call the office back in Miami I decided and update them as to what had happened. Calling the owner of the company I worked for on my brick of a cell phone that I had back then, I told him what had happened and for the second time that day, I boiled up and got extremely pissed off as my boss said, "You aren't going to cancel the boat trip for this afternoon, it is full", knowing he was not thinking about the passengers, but about the revenue, I yelled into the phone, "We just had someone FU%@ing die on us this morning", to which he said "I know, I know".

After a long breath, I told my boss I was canceling this afternoon's boat tour, but rescheduling it for tomorrow so he should not see any loss of revenue from that as of this moment, all tours for the rest of the cruise would go on as normal which I could tell over the phone, made my boss happy.

That night, Becky and I headed off the ship for some dinner (not ship food) and some drinks. As we were walking through the terminal, we saw the wife of the victim with the ships local agent. She had luggage with her and she was obviously leaving the ship to stay with her husband's body. We had found out by this time that they had pronounced the man dead on arrival with a preliminary cause of a massive heart attack. I looked at the wife and she looked at me, it was a strange moment as our eyes locked and she knew who I was and I who she was. To this day I do not know what she was feeling as we looked at each other. I wondered if she was mad at me, but after a moment, she looked away and followed the ships agent to the waiting taxi for the trip back to Hamilton.

The next day, Becky took the boat snorkeling trip out, and I took another tour back to the same beach the man had died the day before as we had that scheduled as well. It was somewhat surreal as we setup on the beach, and I started giving my snorkeling instructions to the group, who all knew what had happened the day before there. One passenger asked me if it was strange being back there after what had a happened and I just looked at him and said, "Yes, Yes it is".

We did our jobs and went on with our lives and finished the week with good sales, and actually good comments despite having a death on one of our tours. On our next trip back to Bermuda, we had to go back to the police station as they had requested us to do to find out what the cause of death was, they told us it was a massive stroke and that was the reason the man never yelled for help, as he literally took his last breath from the snorkel, and was dead.

To be honest, I was upset it had happened, but not really shocked. It was known to me from the beginning of being a Scuba Instructor, snorkel instructor, dive master or whatever you want to call what I had being doing for a living for years now, was that it was not a question of "IF" it would happen, it was a question of when it would happen. The longer you do it and the more people you take on tours in the water, the more likely it will finally happen, and it finally happened to me.

That event caused a little bit of a change in me as I felt like my days of being a water sports guy was coming to an end. I still loved being in the water, but I had been there, done that, and that, and that, and so on. Even Scuba diving was not much fun for me when I was taking people on tours as I felt I was responsible (which I was) for them, and thus, that took some of the joy of being under water away. I loved diving by myself, which is a no no, but it was truly the only time I could actually feel the underwater ZEN I used to know and love before doing Scuba diving and watersports for a living.

It had been an interesting summer aboard the Royal Majesty, I had finally got "out of the Caribbean" as I had only been working there during my time on ships (except for 3 months I spent based out of Los Angeles, but since I was from there, it just seemed liked working at home). We had gotten to explore our home port of Boston which is a great history and "walking" city, got to know the "joy" of dealing with Bermuda customs and immigration and had a death on a tour. We were ready for it to be over, but we did not know when we would be getting off the Royal Majesty, but our Bermuda season of stories was not over, but just about to begin.

A few more cruises went by and we really got to enjoy Bermuda with some great weather, good sales and generally nice passengers (most of our passengers were from the North East, so lots of people from New York, Maine, Rhode Island etc…). Then, one night on our way back to Boston from a great cruise in Bermuda, our cruise came to a sudden stop, literally, we came to a stop. It was about 11:00PM at night and I had just gone to bed as the turnaround day in Boston was always busy from sun up to sun down, when all of a sudden, the intercom in our cabin came to life and we heard an announcement from our Cruise Director. We heard, "Good evening ladies and gentlemen, this is Sammy your Director, we just wanted to inform you that the Royal Majesty has run aground and that we are not in any danger and the ship is working to free itself…….", something like that at least.

I leaped out of bed and got my suit on and headed straight to the bridge. Why you ask would I go to the bridge, well, it was somewhat customary for the dive manager on the ship to offer any assistance when the ship was in trouble, like running aground. So I come up to the door to the bridge panting and trying to catch my breath and I hit the doorbell so to speak, it is a two way intercom with video surveillance so they can see who is at the door. To be honest, I did not expect them to answer the door and was just getting ready to turn around and leave, when the door flew open and one of the Greek officers literally pulled me into the bridge and hurriedly told me to go and sit on the couch on the starboard side of the bridge.

Over I went and sat on the dark bridge as I looked over at the Captain who was in his slippers and yelling loudly about in Greek and officers were scurrying about at his orders. Not much was really happening that I could see as we were not moving at all which made sense as the announcement said we had run aground. After about 20 minutes or so, I figured they did not need me, and they had not offered me any coffee or a cappuccino, so I got up and went over to one of the officers who was not doing anything and told him that if the Captain needed me, to call me to the bridge over the ships intercom and I left the bridge leaving the loud Greek yelling behind me.

Deep down I was relieved, the last thing I wanted to do was to get in the dark water next to ship whose bow was aground, and the back of the ship was still in some unknown depth of water, that and the fact the water near Boston was cold and all I had was a shorty thin wetsuit which only covered part of my arms and down to the length of a pair of shorts, not exactly the appropriate wetsuit to dive into the New England waters. Of course if they would have told me to, I would have gone into the water without thinking about it.

I went out to the open decks to have a look over the side of the ship and also to see how the passengers were handling the situation. Looking down over the side to the water below, I looked forward and could see barely see the bulbous bow sticking out of the water more than it should be. About that time a passenger came running out on the deck wearing their life jacket and looking quite frantic. As much as I wanted to say something to them, my sarcasm was not what that person needed at the moment, but luckily another passenger had no problem laughing at the life jacket clad passenger and yelled with a New England accent, "we are aground, we couldn't sink if we wanted to".

This situation was definitely not like the Titanic as we literally could not sink as the passenger had yelled. I headed toward the stern (back) of the ship to see what I could see there. The farther aft I went, the more vibrations I felt beneath my feet as the deck rumbled more and more. The ship was putting the engines in reverse trying to get the ship free from the sand that it had impaled itself on. When I reached the stern the vibration was incredible, but no matter how much they tried, the ship would not budge and stayed stuck on a beautiful moon lit calm night off of Nantucket.

Having been in situations before where the ship was helpless I knew what to do, and that was to head to the bar. The ship had opened the bars on the ships for free drinks for the passengers so they were packed and there was no way we would get a drink in any of the public bars, so we headed down to the crew bar. No one was sleeping anywhere on the ship with all the excitement of running aground and the crew bar was no exception.

After getting a round of drinks we settled in front of the TV which had CNN on and we were all chatting about our current situation when all of a sudden on CNN there is a picture of the Royal Majesty. They already had a helicopter out over the ship and were doing a live shot of the "drama at sea". I went over to the port hole, looked out and saw the helicopter, then looked back to the TV to the live shot. That was kind of surreal seeing your ship on a live TV feed and being able to look up at the helicopter that was taking the shot.

Seeing us on the news made me think of my parents and what they might think when they looked at the news and saw their son's ship stranded on a sandbar so I headed back to my cabin and grabbed my brick of a cell phone, sat by my port hole and turned it on. To my surprise I got a signal as we were not far from Nantucket.

They answered the phone and I told them that when the look at the news and see my ship is stranded and aground, not to be worried that we were ok. It was an interesting phone call to say the least, but at least they would not worry.

Sometime during the evening or in the morning, the Coast Guard came out with a helicopter and lowered some Coast Guard people onto the helicopter deck on the bow and they went straight to the bridge and basically took over the ships operations with regards to the ships safety. A plan was devised to bring out some tug boats to pull the ship off the sandbar, but those tug boats would not be able to reach the ship until the next evening or so.

There were some ferries based in Nantucket, so someone came up with the idea of using the ferries to take all the passengers (and their luggage) to shore and get them back to Boston via busses. So the order was given for all passengers to put their luggage outside their door for them to be picked up as they normally would the last night of the cruise. The poor cabin stewards had to collect all the luggage and get it all ready to be transferred to the ferries along with the passengers.

The time and the ferries had come to get the passengers off our stuck in the mud (sand) ship. I was on the gangway to lend any help I could to the process and watched as the first ferry motored up alongside us. The seas were calm, but there a small swell of seas that would make it tough on the ferries. They could only come up to the ship on the starboard (right) side, as the Royal Majesty was listing (leaning) slightly to starboard so the port (left) side of the ship could not be used at that angle. As the first ferry approached, it was moving left and right a lot with the slow wide waves of the sea. When it was a few feet away, the swaying stopped a little and it came up next to the ship with not so soft thump.

They attempted to attach lines from the ferry to the ship to secure them together for a safe traverse for the passengers from the ship to the ferry. But within a minute or so, the ferry got pulled away from the ship by the swell, and then back it came and violently "slammed" against the side of the Royal Majesty. At almost the instant we heard the sound of the ships banging together, we heard a loud explosion of what turned out to be the glass windows on the ferry exploding.

Immediately what loose lines there were connecting the two ships were undone and the ferry gunned its engine in reverse and pulled back along the Royal Majesty as it scraped along the stern and finally was clear of the ship. It could not go forward as if it did, it would get stuck on the sandbar the same as the Royal Majesty was.

At that moment the Coast Guard personal that was in charge of the situation looked to the Staff Captain and said, "That was a good try", and then just walked away. It was obvious to all who were on the gangway right then that plan A did not work. So the announcement went out for all passengers to return to their cabins and their luggage would be returned as soon as it could be returned. The passengers were not going anywhere this day or this evening and they started working on plan B.

As for the conditions, I cannot say they were bad. Everything on the ship was pretty much in working order so we had food, water and toilets and electricity. The only difference than being in port was that the ship listed (leaned) to starboard and through the day you got used to correcting for the listing as your body leaned itself to the left to keep yourself up straight when walking towards the front of the ship.

There were not many updates, so it was hurry up and wait most of the day. Plan B appeared to be waiting for the fleet of tug boats that were on their way to use to see if they could pull us off the sandbar. Later in the day the tugs arrived, but nothing seemed to happen and we all were waiting for the ship to move violently or something. And then it finally happened, around 10:00PM, I was walking around and I noticed my body did not have to lean anymore to compensate for the listing of the ship. The tug boats had pulled us off the sandbar and we were floating again.

The ship quietly got under way after some internal hull inspections. The rumor was we sustained some damage to the bottom of the ship, but that the Coast Guard had pronounced that we were able to make it Boston, so we slowly headed to our home port. The next morning the passengers disembarked the ship and it was strange to have the ship be empty. I believe we were there for a day or two before the decision was made to head to New Port News ship yards in Virginia to go into dry dock for them to repair the hull.

As this story comes to a conclusion, you must be asking yourself, "Self, how does a large cruise ship with all the modern navigation equipment go aground on a sandbar that has been on the charts since the 1800's on a clear, moonlit night and the sandbar was lighted with buoys to show where it was, well, this is how it was explained to me by the ships officers.

On that cruise when we were heading to Bermuda, the GPS was giving a beep or some kind of error, but still seemed to be working. None of the ships officers could figure out what the error was telling them, and it seemed to be working normally. The Captain had them compare the reading on where we were with the old system called Loran which is based upon buoys in the ocean and is not nearly as accurate as GPS, but the two seemed to be in synch, so we just went on our merry way to Bermuda.

When we left Bermuda on our way back to Boston, the error was still there, but again they checked it against the Loran and all seemed to be ok. The night when the ship went aground, the officer on the bridge was new, as a matter of fact, they said that it was his first night on watch by himself (him and the Pilipino quartermaster who was on the Bridge). The quartermaster, who had spent something like 20 years at sea, told the new officer that the ship was getting into shallow water. The officer went and checked the GPS and it showed they were right on course. After repeated warnings from the quartermaster, the officer told him to be quiet and that he was an officer and knew where they were (imagine that, an arrogant officer).

Well, they kept on course and eventually ended up on the sandbar. The reason why the GPS was wrong, well in a way it was not, it was just doing the best job it could considering the error it had.

And the error that they could not figure out was that the GPS was no longer receiving information from the satellites. I was told that the wire in the back of the GPS unit that was the connection to the GPS antennae was pulled out a little and was not making contact. Instead of the GPS just shutting down, it was taking all the information it was getting about the ship's speed and direction from the other ships systems, and it was doing its best to "guess" where the ship was. The further the ship traveled, the more "off course" the ship got.

There is a big life lesson in this story. As for the officers, the new officer was fired and the Captain resigned. Funny thing was that a few months later, that Captain got a new job with Celebrity cruise lines and was the Captain of a bigger and newer ship than the Royal Majesty. You have to love it when that happens.

The next few cruises were somewhat uneventful compared to some that summer, and Becky and I found out that our services were needed elsewhere for the company. They told us that the couple who had replaced us on the S/S Seabreeze were not doing well and had pissed off the ships senior management and that the ship wanted them gone and that they were not very happy with our company. My boss told the ship they would bring back Guy and Becky which much to my surprise, they really wanted us back even after all the drama we went through on our first contract on the Seabreeze, but apparently they liked us.

The company wanted us to finish out the Bermuda season which was only a few more weeks, then we would go straight to the S/S Seabreeze and take over there for who knows how long (it turned out to be a long contract). That was fine with me and Becky, we liked the Royal Majesty, but were ready to leave. And after the next cruise, we could not leave fast enough.

There was a hurricane brewing in the Atlantic and was heading for Bermuda. This made going to Bermuda out of the question, and the only two options were for the ship to head north to Maine and maybe Quebec, or to head south and go to the Bahamas. Since the hurricane was not near the US East coast, it was decided to head to the Bahamas, so south we went. It was a great break for us as we only had one snorkeling tour scheduled in Nassau, and no tours setup in Grand Bahama, so even though it would mean no money (since we were paid on commission), we would treat it as a quick working vacation.

The weather down to the Bahamas was nice, while we were there it was the perfect island days and we had a good time and got to relax and organize ourselves a little before signing off the ship in a few weeks. Then there was the trip back to Boston, or so we thought we were going to Boston. The hurricane had diverted from its predicted course and had traveled closer to shore, imagine that, a weather forecast that was not accurate.

Basically the hurricane was between the Bahamas and Bermuda and although we would not need to head into the heart of the storm, we would have to travel through the Westward bands. Damn the torpedoes as they say and we headed to Boston while hugging the East Coast to try and get as far away from the effects of the hurricane as we could which costs us to go slower than anticipated for the cruise.

Even though we hugged the East Coast, we were taking a beating from really rough seas and high winds. The ship was being tossed about like a cork and it was actually much worse than other ships I had been on because the ship had somewhat of a flat hull. The original design of the ship was as a car carrier/cruise ship to operate in Europe, but after a bankruptcy the hull was sold and the ship finished being built as a cruise ship for Majesty Cruise Lines. So the ship's bow would go up on a big angle, then when the water beneath it was gone, the ship basically crashed down back to the ocean and since the hull was somewhat flat, it was like it was doing a belly flop every time it came back down.

The feeling was like going up, up up, then down, down, and crash and the whole ship would just shake violently until it went back up again. The sound it was making was incredible. Down our hallway, every time the ship did its belly flop, the sounds was like Arnold Schwarzenegger with a big metal trash can in each hand and slamming the two together as hard as he could. Now this was a cruise just after the ship's hull had been repaired in dry dock from when it ran aground. We all wondered if our flat bottom ship could take a pounding like this after the damage it had sustained weeks before.

We were informed that we would arrive late into Boston, but they could not say how much. This made our New England passengers not very happy to say the least. Then there was a "meeting" of sorts for all the passengers to be held in the main lounge and hosted by the Cruise Director. He announced that the ship would not be able to make back to Boston, but would be going to New York Harbor instead and they would be bussed back to Boston. It was a mad house when that was announced and people started screaming and a few tried to "rush" the stage, but they had anticipated that and had security ready to intercept them. One elderly man appeared to have a heart attack and they had to call a Code Alpha (medical emergency) and take him to the ship's hospital.

Now although I said that we had had a good cruise in the Bahamas, what I did not tell you is that the passengers were pissed off from the time they got on the ship and found out we were not going to Bermuda, and got madder and madder with each day of the cruise. They were incredibly rude to the crew and were about the worst passengers I had ever had. When we were in Nassau, the Shore Excursion Manager was on the pier using a payphone to call home when a passenger literally pulled her out of the phone booth, hung up the phone and then started making their own phone call and saying that she did not deserve to use the phone (with their heavy New England accent).

Needless to say these people were not our favorites. They defiantly were not good at taking lemons and making lemonade as this whole cruise had been about making the best of a not perfect situation, and although I felt bad the trip they had planned was not the one they were getting, but that does not excuse treating people poorly.

Later that day the ship had to put security at the purser's desk as some of the guests were trying to jump the counter to get at the ships staff who was not telling them what they wanted to hear.

The ship itself was like a refugee camp as no one wanted to be in their cabins in the extremely rough seas. Families had blankets here and there and made makeshift camps all over the interior of the ship, down the hallways that were near windows, in the lounges, you name it. The only place they were not was out on the open decks as those had been closed off due to the high winds we were in.

Luckily for me I have never been sea sick in my life, that is not a macho statement, but the motion of the ocean has never bothered me. I walked around the ship and saw all these people in misery, grown men laying on the floor and some even crying. People with bad motion sickness say that at first you think you are going to die, then you afraid you aren't going to die and you have to suffer through it. Normally I would have been very sympathetic to the passengers, but due to their bad behavior, I walked around and just laughed to myself.

The worse scene I saw on this cruise had to be when I was walking to take the large staircase to another deck and someone had vomited on the stairs, and since they were open stairs, the vomit was dripping down between the stairs to the stairs below them and so on (gross I know).

We finally arrived in New York Harbor which was exciting for me as it was my first time in New

York City and I pretty much had some time off and went and saw the Empire State building and other sites we were able to get to in a few hours of walking around Manhattan. As for the passengers, they got on busses either to a New York airport to catch a flight home, or if they had driven to the port of Boston, they were bussed there, which for some who drove to Boston from New York meant taking a bus up, and then driving back to the same place where the ship was, ouch!!!!

It was a great day in New York and as we left later in the evening because they had to bus the people down from Boston for the next cruise and as we left the port that night passing the Statue of Liberty, there was fireworks show off in the distance somewhere and it made for one of my most memorable sail aways ever.

As for me and Becky, it was our last cruise to Bermuda (I would end up going back to Bermuda almost ten years later after a refit of a ship, that story is coming up later in the book), and we flew down to Miami to get back on board the S/S Seabreeze for turned out to be the next 9 months.

You can check out photos of the Royal Majesty & Bermuda at www.CruiseShipStories.com

Even though I was happy when we had left the Seabreeze all those few months ago, I was glad to be back on board her. There was a familiarity to the ship with regards to knowing your way around, and also the people. It seemed like most of the crew we had worked with were still there. Some had gone on vacation and come back, but there were enough of them that it somehow felt like family and we looked forward to this next contract.

It was not long after we were back to our usual Eastern one week, Western Caribbean the next routine. Once again it was in Grand Cayman where I got to do something I had not really done before and that was to secure the bow thruster of the Seabreeze as it was not working. The Captain had called me, yes my favorite Captain whom I had had my situations I wrote about earlier in the book. He informed me that the bow thruster had broken and it was "free spinning" which was causing it more damage and that I needed to secure it so it would not move until they could have it fixed.

The bow thruster is basically a tube going through the hull in the front of the ship with a single propeller in that could push the front of the ship left or right (to the port or starboard) when maneuvering in port. They had some divers and a boat from Grand Cayman they had hired to help with the securing of it, one of whom I had known from when I lived on Grand Cayman.

We got our gear we were going to use to secure the propeller and hopped on the dive boat from the gangway and headed to the bow of the ship. Since the bow thruster is only a few feet under the water line, it did not take us long to get into it and get to work. One nice thing about working in a bow thruster was that you could set your tools down on the bottom of the tunnel which made things easier.

I know this story is not that exciting so let me get to the part that makes the story somewhat worthy of being in this book. First, it is not every day you get to work on a bow thruster on a ship floating off an island, especially since modern ships now have grates on each side entrance to the thruster tunnel so you could not really work on them at seas nowadays, and second was when we all almost crapped our wetsuits.

We'd been taking out time setting up how we would secure it and after about 45 minutes of not moving much and hooking cables up to it, all of sudden there was the loudest siren I had ever heard go off underwater. Now for those of you who aren't Scuba or water people, let me tell you that sound travels extremely well and far underwater and it is almost impossible to figure out where the sound is coming from.

We all froze and stopped what we were doing and starred at each other through our masks as we pondered what could they be telling us with that siren, was the ship about to get moving, if so, I would not want to be in the bow thruster tunnel when it starts moving. So we literally dropped our tools and each headed out of the tunnel, the other two divers were on the side of the tunnel where the dive boat was, I was on the opposite side so I left the tunnel and then dived under the bow and back over to the other side to the dive boat and surfaced where the other divers had.

We asked the Greek officer on the boat what the hell was going on and he responded he had no idea what we were talking about and he contacted the ship with his UHF radio to see if anything was wrong. After some yelling back and forth in Greek over the radio, he shrugged his shoulders and told us nothing was wrong and to get back to work.

Finishing the job we were cold and tired after being underwater for about ninety minutes and he headed back to the dive boat and then to the ship. The Staff Captain took us to a lounge and bought us a Hot Coffee with Whiskey in it to warm us up, that was all I got paid for that diving expedition. I really did not care I had not got paid as I did a favor for the Captain and the ship, and got to dive in a bow thruster while a ship was drifting off of Grand Cayman. Not the most exciting story I know, but it was a good memory for me.

It was a few weeks later when again I was called upon to dive under the ship, but this time it was for a completely unrelated reason to the ships maintenance. This was for a passenger. I was called to the gangway while we were in St. Thomas, I had done my snorkeling tours earlier in the day and was relaxing before having to go and work at the dive desk that evening.

The Greek officer on the gangway led me to a couple whom the woman had dropped the plastic part of her wallet containing all her id's and credit cards over the side of the ship while on the gangway. To shorten the story, I get my scuba gear, jump off the pier closest to the gangway which was about a fifteen foot drop to the water. I swim to underneath the gangway where the woman said she was and froze and just let myself go with current and sink as the plastic case that she had lost I assume would have done.

Well let's hear it for dumb luck, I practically landed on the plastic case when I reached the bottom. It was too short to go back to the surface so soon, I had to make it look like it took me some time and effort to find it, so I decided to take a tour of the side of the ship, and what I saw made my eyes go big in my mask. It was amazing to me that the distance from the sand under the side of the ship on the starboard side where we were docked in St. Thomas was only a few inches, literally. I could barely get my hand between the sand and the side of the ship. That seemed just too close for comfort, but they knew what they were doing I guess.

Back on the surface, I told them I had found what the passenger had lost, and I took off my Scuba gear and floated there while they lowered a rope down to me in the water. I attached the rope to my gear and the large bulky bear of a Greek Officer lifted my gear out of the water and up to the dock. There were no ladders anywhere around for me to get out, so the officer said he would pull me up with the rope like he had just done with my gear.

So I wrapped the rope around my right hand a few times to make sure it would not slip, and had planned to use my left hand to actually hold the rope, but the when the officer saw I had the rope he "yanked" on it and I felt like Superman as I flew straight up and out of the water with one hand above my head and my right hand wrenched with pain as the rope tightened around it with my weight.

Before I knew it I was up on dock and quickly untied the rope from my hand to see a red, and already bruising hand. The passengers were thankful and gave me a hundred dollar bill for my efforts which I appreciated, but no good deed goes unpunished. It took months for my hand to get back to fully functional and just worked with the pain until it was healed.

It does not happened often, but sometimes a passenger has to be taken off a ship by a helicopter due to a medical emergency, and on the newer ships it can be easier since they all have helicopter pads, but on the old Seabreeze, there was no option for that so they had to do it the old fashion way, and that was to hover over the ship. We were in the Caribbean and luckily it was a nice calm day with a light breeze. A passenger had had a heart attached and the Coast Guard had sent out a helicopter to get them back to shore for proper medical attention.

Why am I telling a story about a helicopter evacuation from a ship, well you will see in a moment why. The helicopter hovered over the stern (back) of the ship and lowered one of its crew to the deck, they got the man in the basket and hoisted him up to the helicopter. While this was going on, I was on one of the upper decks of the ship and it was a strange view as I was looking straight out at the front of the helicopter at almost the same height, I could see the pilot concentrating on keeping his aircraft in the right spot as the ship moved slowly forward in the seas.

It seemed like everyone was out on deck with their cameras out and taking photos of the event like you assume people would do. Well in a few minutes it was over and the helicopter was off to shore. Later that night I dropped by the photo gallery to see my friend the Chief Photographer. Out of the corner of my eye, I see a woman frantically snatching up photos from the wall and I think how they are about to make a good sale.

But upon closer look, I see the woman is taking the photos off the wall of the man who was evacuated by helicopter. These pictures were close up of the man, with an ashen face, oxygen mask on and in the basket that he was hoisted to the helicopter on. What the hell I thought, and I go over to the Turkish ships photographer who was working the photo gallery. I asked him why in the world he has photos of that man for sale to which he replies in his thick Turkish accent, "If they want to buy them, they can buy them".

Horrified I race over the ship to look for the Chief Photographer, and finally find him and let him know what his photog was selling in his photo gallery. He raced down to get them off the wall and refund the woman who was buying them as she was the wife of the victim. Needless to say this was a topic at the weekly Captains management meeting and the Chief Photographer had some explaining to do.

Earlier in the book I mentioned about being able to work with some great comedians and some of the ones on the Seabreeze were fantastic. That ship usually had comedians stay on for months at a time, just to do one main show a week, talk about a good gig.

One of these comedians became good friends with many of us crew and we would go every week to see his show, even though it was the same show every week. It was going to be his last show and we wanted to send him off with a bang, so the staff got together and came up with a way to give him a sendoff during his final performance for that contract.

During his show, he would do a bit about the seven short and one long blast on the ships horn that they used when there is an emergency. The passengers are familiar with it as the ship blasted its horn seven short and one long before we left Miami when we did the passenger life boat drill. So the comedian begins his bit for this, and puts his mouth to the microphone and does him impersonation of the seven short and one long blast and while his is doing that, about ten of us staff race out of every entrance to the lounge wearing our life jackets and holding our paddles to show where the emergency stations are just like we did during the passenger drill.

We all had panicked looks on our faces as we entered the lounge from six different locations, (this lounge had two stair wells in the lounge, so you could enter it from the deck below) and headed toward the stage. The passengers looked as us wondering what was going on, and as we looked on stage, there we saw our comedic friend looking at us with his mouth open.

It was quite for a moment as we looked at the comedian to see what he would do, and he finally put the microphone to his mouth and told everyone in the lounge that for the first time in his career, he was speechless. He then went on to say how much the crew had been like family to him and the ship was like another home. This is just nice story to show how even on a ship, you can have fun with people you like, even in front of hundreds of paying passengers.

We worked the ship for over six months and even though the ship felt like family, it was a job I knew and loved and the money was actually pretty good, but I knew it was time to move on, and not from just from the Seabreeze, but from what I was doing for a living.

There were plenty more questions than answers when it came to what I would do with my life next, and then there was Becky, whatever I did had to include her, but how? After a lot of thinking and going over different options, which included going back to live on land and get a "real job", but that idea was quickly tossed out of the options box, I (we) decided it was time to get out of diving and stop working for concessions who contracted with cruise lines and instead to work for an actual cruise line.

I sent out my resume to the major cruise lines to apply to be with Shore Excursions, this way I could leverage my excursion experience, but would not have to take people on the actual tours like I had been doing for years. The idea was for me to get a job, and then I would get Becky hired, a risk for sure, but nothing is gained if you don't try. This time it was a little easier as I asked my tour operators throughout the Caribbean who was the people I should contact at each of the cruise lines I was applying to, so at least I had a name and a phone number.

After I sent out my resumes, it was time to start the phone calling (and calling and calling). I got through to most and they said they would have a look, but as it was with Shore Excursions, they usually promoted from within their own ranks, meaning they did not hire outside the company directly to a Shoe Excursion position. The cruise line I wanted to work for the most was Royal Caribbean and thus most of my attention (phone calls) went to them, and since the S/S Seabreeze's home port was the Port of Miami and the offices for Royal Caribbean were just a few minutes' walk from my ship, I thought it would easier to get an interview.

It took weeks of phone calls (polite bugging), but Royal Caribbean finally agreed to interview me for a Shore Excursion position. Luck was on my side at that time as the Seabreeze was in wet dock in the Port of Miami. Wet dock is when a ship going out of service for maintenance, but unlock dry dock, it stays in the water tied to the pier during this time. I went to the interview and the Royal Caribbean Shore Excursion shore side manager was a very nice woman who told me how they never hired people directly to an excursion position, but they had agreed to my interview as they did not have many good internal candidates for shore excursion positions which I found hard to believe since they had over 20 ships and thousands upon thousands of crew members in their fleet, but I was happy they had that problem.

During the interview I gave her my resume, and then a page of recommendation from people I had worked with for years throughout the Caribbean, but she did not really need my pages of recommendations as she said, "I have already called around about you". When I heard that I was taken off guard for a moment, not that I was worried about what people would say, but was taken aback that she had gone to the effort to make phone calls to her tour operators to see if they knew me. The interview went well and I was given an application to fill out and all in all I felt like I had a chance at getting a job as an Assistant Shore Excursion manager with Royal Caribbean Cruise lines.

The day after my interview, the Seabreeze was back online and going on its first cruise after the wet dock. It was an interesting week to say the least and here is what happened. Since back then we did not have internet or anything like that, it was still just phone calls through satellites and faxes through satellites (and both were really expensive). Not wanting to wait to mail my application to Royal Caribbean, I paid the money and gave my application to the Seabreeze's radio officer to fax my application into Royal Caribbean. I knew the radio officer would read my application as that was his job, he read every incoming and outgoing fax as back then the Captain wanted to know all information leaving his ship and coming into his ship, that was just the way it was, but that would change soon when the internet arrived on ships and they got rid of the radio officer's position which was somewhat replaced by computer systems administrators and the Captains lost the ability to control the information to and from his ship.

As we reached ports and I was conducting my tours, my tour agents all came to me and would say something like, "guess who called me about you", and thus I got to hear about what Royal Caribbean had asked them about me and what they had said. They teased me and said, "don't worry, we lied for you" and laughed and they all told me how great Royal Caribbean was and I would be great doing Shore Excursions on their ships.

It was four days into our seven day cruise when I got the hallway phone call from the radio officer that I had a fax and to come and pick it up in the radio room. After climbing seven decks of stairs, I got to the radio room where the officer handed me my envelope with my fax. I was walking down the hall back to my cabin and opening up my fax to read it and then I had to stop walking and re-read what I thought was in the fax. Yep, there it was, my offer letter from Royal Caribbean Cruise lines to be an assistant Shore Excursion manager and asking me to call them the next time I was in port to setup when I would start work.

To say I was happy was an understatement. I was really excited to get out of diving, but still be able to sell watersports tours, and even more excited to actually work for a cruise line and not a concession where you never knew when they might lose their contract with that cruise line (been there, done that). Becky was also excited with the anticipation of her going to work for a large cruise line and thus the celebration started, for a few minutes that is as by the time I finished telling Becky about the fax and offer letter, I got another hallway phone call, this time it was a bridge officer that told me the Captain wanted to see me in his office immediately, great I thought, what did I do now (I couldn't think of anything).

Entering his cabin saying, "You wanted to see me sir", he said to sit down and I did, with him at his desk just looking at me for a moment. Now this was the same Captain I had "issues" with my past times on the Seabreeze so I never knew what was going to happen with him. He then picks up a piece of paper, appears to read it and sets it down on his desk. I glance down and can see it is a copy of my offer letter from Royal Caribbean Cruise lines and now I know what this call to his office is about.

With his heavy Greek accent, he looks at me and asks, "What's this?" I told him I had been offered a position with Royal Caribbean and that is all I said in reply. He then tells me he had seen my application fax I had sent and he was wondering how they offered me a job so quickly, to which I then told him about the interview during wet dock.

I could go on with the conversion I had with him, but here it is in a nutshell. He was disappointed I had not gone to Dolphin Cruise Lines for a Shore Excursion position and then offered me a position as Shore Excursion Manager on any of the two Dolphin Cruise Lines ships (including the one I was on at that moment). That was a little shocking as I did not expect a pseudo counteroffer, especially from a Captain whom Captains do not hire Shore Excursion managers.

As politely as I could, I told him thank you for the offer, but I really wanted to go and see what I could learn at Royal Caribbean and he shook my hand as we ended the conversion and he said if I ever wanted to come back to Dolphin Cruise lines, to call him which I thought was an incredibly nice offer, especially coming from the Captain of a ship.

The next day in port I called Royal Caribbean and we agreed that I would start work in two weeks and they assigned me to the Sovereign of the Seas which was based out of Miami doing the Eastern Caribbean cruises which was very similar to the cruises I was currently doing on the Seabreeze. I asked Royal Caribbean if I could fly out of St. Thomas so that I could finish my last cruise as that was the last port and I could make some money that week instead of sitting in a hotel in Miami waiting for my new ship, and they said yes. So I finished my last snorkel tour in the morning in St. Thomas, then signed off the ship and headed to the airport to fly to Miami to begin my new adventures with shore excursions, but this time with one of the largest cruise lines and ship's in the world and I wondered what stories I would experience there, well you are about to read some of those stories and experiences.

I would like to stop for a moment and take time to thank you for reading this book thus far. It has been an emotional time reliving some great and not so great times in my life and I am looking forward to sharing the most notable times of the next 6 years of mine on cruise ships. This change was not just a little one, but a defining one in my life. The reason I say that is that until this time, working on ships has been from contract to contract, never really knowing what I wanted to do and not thinking that far ahead. But at this junction I knew I would be on ships for some years to come and that it was now a "real job" for me and one I was perfectly happy and privileged to have. Thanks again and let's get another round of drinks and continue on with the stories and experiences on cruise ships.

Walking onto the gangway of the Sovereign of the Seas was an incredible experience, meaning I felt like I had made it in the cruise ship business, the world was my oyster, anything was possible, and then the crap began to pile up, almost literally.

After doing the normal paperwork to sign onto a ship (those things don't really change no matter what ship or what cruise line you are working on) I headed to my cabin where I knocked, the door opened and I looked out and said, "Hi Steve". Now you may be asking yourself how I knew the name of my cabin mate and here is where after being on ships for years, you start to be in the six degrees of separation for ships meaning you can talk to a crewmember and find out where they have worked and who with, most likely you will both know the same people.

Steve as it happens was the husband of an entertainer who performed regularly on the S/S Seabreeze and he was her technician. As it turned out, the two had gotten a divorce and he took a job as a sound and light technician with Royal Caribbean. It was nice to see a familiar face and made the transition to a new ship (and new cruise line) that much easier for me and made sharing a cabin easier since I had only shared a cabin with Becky the last few years so having a new cabin mate was something new again.

It was Steve's last cruise before going on vacation and I would get a new cabin mate the next day in Miami, which funny as it was, the next week I walked into my cabin, saw someone sitting on the bottom bunk and I said, "Hi Paul". My new cabin mate was another sound and light technician I had worked with, but from my old NCL days, we had both worked on the M/V Southward out of Los Angeles and I had done the lights for the production shows and he was the main tech who ran the show, so another good stroke of luck in the cabin mate department.

As with all things, luck runs out and since Paul was only on the ship for one cruise before being transferred to another ship, the next Miami day I got a new cabin mate, but this one I did not know. He was a young kid in very early 20's and this was his first ship. He was working as a cruise staff member and was excited about being on ships and ya ya ya, you get the idea. His first night on ships was kind of like my first night on ships, but he could not handle it well to say the least. I came home later in the evening after having some drinks with some other crew members I had worked with who were on the Sovereign and there I found this new cabin mate passed out on the lower bunk which was my bunk and at first I kind of laughed at this "newbie" passing out on his first night on ships. But the humor ran off quickly as I opened the bathroom to see a horrible scene like I had never seen.

Put your drink down for a moment as you won't want to drink or eat as I describe this. The tiny bathroom was covered in vomit and to add insult to injury, the toilet was not working as seemed to be the usual case on the Sovereign which I will talk about next. The toilet was filled with crap and vomit and it took everything I could not to add my vomit to what looked like a crime scene. I was pissed off then. Things were not going well on my first ship with the first shore excursion manger I was working with, but we can go over later.

You can pick your drink back up now as I will exclude any more gory details, but the next morning I went to the assistant cruise director and insisted that idiot in my cabin be moved to another cabin. The ACD understood and tried, but could not move the kid to another cabin as was the usual case, the crew cabins were full so I had to put up with him for a few more weeks.

Now onto be on the first ship of a new class of cruise ships can bring on some issues. The Sovereign of the Seas was really the first one labeled a "Mega Ship" and much of the technology put into it was brand new. That included the toilet system. Now vacuum toilets had been around for many years, but not on the scale of this ship, at least at that time. Needless to say the toilets on the Sovereign were constantly plugged up (or the piping was) and they had about four crew members who did nothing but unblock and clear clogged sewer lines that flowed all over the ship. Most places you went on the ship you could at least get a hint of that sewer smell and sometimes it could be overwhelming. They figured out the design issue by the time the second ship in the class (the Majesty of the Seas) came out not long after the Sovereign, but the Sovereign was stuck with its inadequate waste system, but years later in an extensive dry dock they fixed the problem.

Here is a fun note on vacuum toilets, if you are bored or drunk or whatever, here is something to pass the time and make everyone laugh. Pile up a nice wad of toilet paper and put it in the toilet bowl in your cabin. Then gingerly roll out the paper out of the bathroom, then you can either put it all over your cabin, or let it go out down the hall as far as you want. Make sure the bowl of the toilet is dry and is the floor as you don't want it sticking anywhere. When you are ready, flush the toilet and stand back and see that long highway of toilet paper quickly get sucked into the toilet like it was being sucked into a black hole, which it kind of is when you think about it. I digress, back to life and stories on ships.

As excited as I was about being on the Sovereign, it had been a long time since I had worked for someone else, excluding the Cruise Director whom I usually reported to. For the first few weeks I thought I had lost my ability to work for someone as my manager was not a very nice person to work for. She was a new Shore Excursion Manager and I guess wanted to show how she could do it. One of the things the people who hired me told me to do was to learn as much as I could as fast as I could with the hint that there would be bigger and better things to come for me.

So I took that to task and worked day and night to learn the tours, the procedures and the computer systems to sell shore excursions. I also worked a lot as I did not like my cabin mate so I did not want to be there at all so I engulfed myself with being the best assistant shore excursion manager I could be. Things were somewhat tense between myself and the manager as it seemed like she did not want to have anything to do with me and it finally came to a head one night when I was asking her about a particular feature of one of the computer reports and she looked at me and said, "that is not your concern, you are just a little assistant and you only have to worry about selling the tours at the desk and doing what I tell you to do".

Oh I said, and walked out of the office to go about my business. Now I was somewhat deflated as I had worked very hard to learn what I could, but with the manager was not wanting to show me anything, that was a problem to complete what my shore side managers had wanted me to do with learning all I could about the operations of shore excursions.

Royal Caribbean had a dive team on board their ships in the Caribbean, and I had befriended the lead diver on the Sovereign as he once was an interview diver back at NCL and we got along well, so I used him to vent my frustrations with my manager and my current situation (this will have significance as you will soon read). Now I don't know what happened to my manager, but all of a sudden they said she was leaving and going on vacation before her scheduled date, good for me I thought.

They brought on a retired Shore Excursion Manager whom I will call Tex. He was great, and older gentlemen who was also a parrot head and put up a Jimmy Buffet poster in his cabin. He showed me everything I need to know about operations in just the first week of working with him. He also taught me something else, how to manage tour dispatches (the meeting and sending off excursions).

One night we were in San Juan, Puerto Rico and dispatching the night time tours. We had just finished manning the excursion desk and I said I was going to run down to the pier to help dispatch the tours, that is when Tex says, let's go get a beer. "What about the tours", I asked, and he said, "The radio works from the bar". So we went to a lounge, ordered a drink and dispatched the tours via radio with the crew staff who were on the pier. A revelation I thought, and the job got done and everyone was happy.

For years to come when someone called me over the radio and asked where I was, it was not uncommon for me to say I was at my "pier side office", which to my managers and those who knew me meant a bar on the pier. I spent many a day and night dispatching my tours from a bar and though that may sound like I was slacking, you have to understand that it was a way for me not to burn out. On a port day, I could easily work from 6:00AM to well into the night and if you did that all the time and did not delegate and let people do their jobs (like the staff assigned to dispatch the tours), then you would burn out. So I found ways to relax while working and get the job done and done well I might add as all my reviews over the years were nothing but stellar and as you will read, I eventually became one of the "Legends" as our bosses called after being on ships for so long, we of course referred to ourselves as "dinosaurs", but that was later in my Shore Ex career.

I guess you would like a story or two at this point and one from the Sovereign comes to mind. There was a Captain named Captain Johnny, a great Captain and a very nice man, but his one obsession at the time was golf. He golfed in every port that he could and one of the best on this route in the Eastern Caribbean was in Puerto Rico. One cruise we were late getting into San Juan and Captain Johnny was going to miss his tee time if we did not get in soon. So I was on the outside promenade deck as we were backing into the pier and I could not believe how fast we were going. Really, it was like we were cruising at sea, except I stood there watching the pier literally fly by the ships railing as we backed in. Then all of a sudden the ship started to shake and shudder violently and we kind of slowed, but really just came to a sudden stop in perfect position to tie up the ship to the pier.

Moments later I saw Captain Johnny run off the just tied up gangway to his taxi to take him to the golf game. Later I heard from one of the officers that were on the bridge when we arrived that the port pilot was yelling to slow down as we were coming in, but you never want to stop a Captain from making his golf game.

Things were going pretty well on the Sovereign, but I still did not like the ship for some reason. It is strange, although the ship was nice and big, it had a weird strange vibe that did not set well with me and to this day I do not know why. I had only been on board a month or so, but in some ways it had seemed like forever and in other ways it seemed like only a few days.

One night I got called to the Cruise Directors cabin along with Shore Ex Tex and I was wondering what was going on as nothing of distinction had happened, at least that I knew about. We go into the Cruise Directors cabin and we see that he is obviously drunk, but still working as is the life on cruise ships. He proceeds to raise his voice at me saying how could I go behind his back and say that I did not like the ship to our shore side office, to which I told him I had not expressed any dismay with the ship to my shore side managers.

He kept on how pissed he was and then finally said why this all came about, and that is he had received a transfer for me to go to the Majesty of the Seas and that I got the transfer because shore side found out that I was unhappy on the Sovereign and they did not want to lose me, so they decided to transfer me to another ship. After his yelling stopped, we left the office and I asked Tex if he had said anything to which he said he had not.

Then I ran into my diver buddy and told him what had happened and he just looked at me and smiled and said, "Your welcome". I would have loved to see the look on my own face when he said that as I must have looked like a deer in headlights. He went on to tell me how he had gone to my shore side bosses whom he knew very well and told them how well I was doing at my job and that I was not happy on the Sovereign (or the Suffering of the Seas as some of us called it) and thus they decided to move me to a ship where I might be happier. Needless to say that was a strange thing for shore side to consider me and not just the company, I guess I did get the right job with the right people after all.

So off to the Majesty of the Seas I went which was doing the Western Caribbean route (Jamaica, Grand Cayman, Labadee (one of Royal Caribbean's private islands) and Cozumel) which was my overall favorite route.

You might be wondering at this point, what happened to Becky (or maybe you aren't thinking that because you don't care, either way here it is). Since going to Royal Caribbean I was working on getting her a job as cruise staff as that is what she wanted to do and it is also something that she would be great at with her bubbly personality. It was a drama to say the least as they were giving me the runaround and were hiring new cruise staff members with no ship experience and Becky would have been much better at that job so I thought it might be time to think of a plan B for us getting to work together again.

As much as I loved my job and the Majesty of the Seas, the plan was for Becky and I to work and live together soon. We knew it would be a big challenge and a risk, but nothing is gained without taking some risk. So I called up the dive management at NCL who I knew from when I worked with NCL and asked if they were hiring any couples for their dive program and they said they were interested. Over a few weeks we spoke on the phone a few times and all seemed to be going well until the person I was talking to at NCL said they could not hire me because of a relationship they had with my boss (business relationship), something about stealing employees.

Then it was a miracle, Becky got a job offer with Royal Caribbean as a cruise staff member, but on a different ship. Well, we were closer to our goal of being together so we thought it was great.

I found out later in my time with RCCL when I was on a business trip in Alaska with my shore side boss and we had a few drinks, she told me that she was talking with her friend from NCL back when I was calling them and he told her, "Guess who called me". Well, she said she told him, "You can't take my Guy Beach away", and thus he would not hire me and she said she had called in a favor with the person who hired the cruise staff and told him to hire Becky as a personal favor.

So we were closer together in that at least we worked for the same cruise line as Becky went to work on the Monarch of the seas which was based out of San Juan, Puerto Rico and a big party boat I had been told. The next step would be to get us on the same ship, but since I did not know how long I was going to be on the Majesty of the Seas, it was difficult to coordinate it, but I was going to actively try and get on the Monarch of the Seas as I thought it would be easier for me to get transferred as compared with Becky who was set to be there 9 months on her first contract.

Out of all of my ships, I believe the Majesty of the Seas to be one of my favorites. Maybe it was because it did the Western Caribbean which was my favorite up to this point. The ship itself was almost identical to the Sovereign of the Seas which I hated. Maybe it was the family type atmosphere on it, who knows, all I knew is I liked the ship, the people and the itinerary.

My first boss the Majesty was a very interesting fellow. He had recently come out of the closet and was now openly gay. I got there just as he had announced that he was switching teams and the whole ship was in shock. Now being gay on a ship is nothing new, a good percentage of the crew was gay or bi or whatever, but this person was a huge womanizer who was known for sleeping with a lot of women on ships and this sudden change took people by surprise.

He was a good manager, taught me more about the ins and outs of being a shore ex manager and he was good to deal with. My cabin was next to his and he partied until late in the evening most nights which did not help my sleep much, but all in all, it was good to work for him.

After a few weeks, the manager had left for another ship and I got a new manager who was "Epic". He was a party boy that loved to drink and loved for you to drink. There was nothing like being woken up at 2:00AM, opening your cabin door and having a bottle of booze shoved in your face and your manager yelling, "Let's drink". Now I like to have fun and all, but this was over the top for me and I had to find ways to politely get out of his nightly binge drinking.

Even though he drank to excess, he always showed up to work on time, maybe hung over, but he showed up. He was a good functional drunk and fit perfectly into ship life.

They liked to do pranks on crew members when on their first ship. Some of the classics were "Fog Watch", where we would send someone out on the bow with binoculars and a hand held radio and tell them to watch for fog and inform the bridge if they saw it. The Captain helped us with this prank as he would tell the crew member how important the job was and then we would look down at them from the bridge as they stood on the bow and chuckle to our own amusement.

Another fun item was when we would be in an office or a cabin hanging out and one of us would ask the other what their electric bill was last month. That usually got the attention of the newbie and we would tell them how expensive it was if you kept your cabin lights on and that they took the money right out of your pay. Yes it was juvenile, but we had fun.

On one of the days I was in Miami, the Seabreeze was there and my old friend the assistant cruise director came on my ship (I got him a day pass). We went to a bar, had a few drinks and got caught up on what was going on the Seabreeze and how things were going on for me at Royal Caribbean. One drink turned to another, then another, then another, well you get the picture. Finally it was time for sail away so my friend went back to his ship and then I got myself the passenger life boat drill we always had just before we left the pier.

I was feeling really really good at the boat drill as you can imagine. So there I was speaking into megaphone to organize the passengers and I turn around and see a video camera pointed at me. It was one of Royal Caribbean's shore side video crew. They kept on filming me as I mustered the passengers, all the while I was thinking, crap, I'm feeling really good right now and I hope it does not show on the video. After the drill I went off to the excursion desk to work and forgot about the video crew from the life boat drill.

It was months later when I signed onto another ship and I had to sit and watch the safety video that one always had to watch upon signing onto a ship, whether you had worked on that ship or not. They came to a part of drinking and how not to drink too much and so on, when all of a sudden, there I am on the video doing the life boat drill those months ago after a few hours at the bar. Oh the irony I thought, I wonder if the video guy put my footage in there on purpose as a joke, I never knew, but as I went from ship to ship the next few years, I always had to watch myself at that drill as they talked about drinking and working and it always brought a smile to my face.

Of course at that point in time, no one really cared about drinking while working, as long as you got your job done and did not embarrass the cruise line or cause a law suit. If only the passengers who went up to the excursion desk to find out about the tours knew that if they went into our back office, the desks back there would be covered with empty glasses as the staff rotated from the front desk, to back office to have a drink. The bar manager would send people over to pick up all the glasses as they were running out of them in the bars. One time the hotel manager walked into our back office on the Majesty on the way to his office, saw the desks covered with empty glasses, looked at me and just shook his head and went to his office. Funny thing is 10 minutes later, I saw a bartender deliver a drink to the hotel manager in his office, so I just shook my head and laughed.

Now one good thing about working on Royal Caribbean was that the ships officers were "international", meaning they were all a mix of mostly European and Scandinavian's and not just one nationality like Norwegian, or Greek or Italian. It was fantastic to say the least. Finally the monopoly or good'ol boys club of the officers was pretty much gone when you have a Norwegian staff captain, a Greek captain and a hodgepodge of everything in between. Don't get me wrong, they still looked after one another, but not in any way close to when they were all from the same country.

Here is a story that I will classify as hearsay or as Cathy Griffin would say, "Allegedly". It went around the entire fleet that a hotel manager on a ship other than the one I was on was fired. Now that happens every now and then, even at that high level, but the reason for this one was hilarious. It appears that the hotel director kept nominating and selecting a particular female crew member as the employee of the month, which on top of the photo you get on the wall, includes a nice bit of cash as a reward. It was suspicious to say the least, but then it was found out (allegedly) that the female crew member was his mistress, and that he kept making her employee of the month every now and then to pay for her abortions as he had knocked her up more than once. That was too much for shore side, so he was gone, and good ridden is what I was told from people who worked for him who stated he was a tyrant and horrible to work for.

I was having a great time on the Majesty, working hard and learning all about managing excursions on Royal Caribbean ships. Then the word came down that I was leaving the Majesty and going to the Nordic Empress, but not as an assistant Shore Excursion Manager, but as THE Shore Excursion Manger. I was being promoted during my first contract with the company which made me feel good, but also the pressure was on to succeed as a manger as they had hired me to become a Shorex manager as soon as possible, and this was sooner than I had expected.

Now I had worked on ships for years by now, and thought I knew most of the things that went on above deck, below decks, in front of the curtain, behind the curtain, you get the idea. There was one aspect that I apparently had worked around for quite some time, but I guess my naivety in this area was about to be known.

First let me talk a little about the history of cruise ships and money. Up until the 1990's, when cruise lines began to go "public" and be a traded stock instead of being privately owned, everyone made money. For example: before the 1990's, a Cruise Director would give a talk to the passengers about the shore excursions available and the cruise line would give him a dollar for every tour he or she sold. Now the tour company that sold the tour would also give the Cruise Director a dollar for each tour they sold. So the Cruise Director would get 2 dollars for every tour they sold (I am using a dollar as an example, each tour had its own dollar amount).

The Cruise Director would also talk to the passengers about where to shop in the ports and tips on what to buy and where the "deals" were. The cruise line did not pay them for this service, but the stores in the ports that the Cruise Director suggested everyone to go shopping sure did. So at the end of the day in port, either the Cruise Director or a crewmember authorized by the

Cruise Director would go around the shops that were "suggested" and would take the payout for that day. One of my friends who had been around in those days told me that on some days the payout could be as much as $10,000 for just one day. Now the Cruise Director would share this loot or bounty with his staff, those who helped him with the selling of those shops and tours.

This went on with just about every part of the ship that dealt with a company in a port. Which company got the contract for taking away the garbage, or supply food and alcohol to the ship was the company that offered the most incentive (kickback) to those working shore side back in Miami and to those who worked on the ships. This was just the way the cruise line industry was and is still somewhat that way today, with some slight differences and variations of the kickback, or at least who gets them.

Back then, everyone knew what was going on and everyone was having a good time and making money so no one cared, not even the owners of the cruise lines as they were making money hand over fist and were not that greedy. Then when the cruise lines started to be public companies being traded in the stock market, everything changed. It all came down to the bottom line and the dividend to the stock holders.

By the time I got to ships, they had Shore Excursion managers who had taken over the selling of the tours from the Cruise Directors, and then later came the port and shopping people who took over the selling of what stores to buy from in the ports of call. Now the money from shore side to the ship kept flowing, it was just much more under the table and shared between the cruise director and others directly involved.

Now in the dive business on ships, there were no kickbacks, at least none that I knew of, but now in the world of Shore excursions, I was going to be exposed to a whole new world, and I really did not like what I saw. My manager on the Majesty sat me down in his cabin and explained how the system worked. I was shocked to say the least. My first thought was I did not want to get fired, but then he explained to me that the system had been setup by all my bosses shore side when they worked on ships before transferring to land in Miami and working in the corporate office.

I was also told not to say anything or to make waves and if I did, I would probably be let go which was easy back then, they just fired you for no good reason and that happened all the time. Now I have to say that the money sounded good, but then again, I did not do this job for the money, I did it because I loved it and this whole side of ships I did not like.

So off I went to the Nordic Empress to be the Shore Excursion manager. It was a relatively new and small ship that did the 3 / 4 day route from Miami to the Bahamas, the same route that I had done for years, so at least I knew the ports. When I got to the ship I was told by the Hotel Director and Cruise Director that I had big shoes to fill as the manager that I replaced was the only one who could "handle" the excursion on that ship. I just nodded and said I would do the best I could, but in the back of my mind was thinking, "how hard can it be", it was like ground hog day, the same thing almost every day and the same ports twice a week.

I found out that the staff who worked for the Excursion manager had hated him, so much to the point that it almost got physical and some wanted to kick his ass. Well, I have an easy going approach to managing and the staff welcomed me with open arms and I treated them well and they worked hard for me. The tour operators like me and we got along well. The number of tours I sold exceeded that of the previous manager, and the negative comments on the tours had gone down as well. So revenue was up, complaints down, and the staff were happy to work with the shore excursion department.

Apparently this is why my bosses shore side sent me there, and that was to prove to Nordic Empress executive staff that the manager before me was not the only one who could run the excursions on that ship, and I passed that test with flying colors.

It was time for vacation and I was going to back to the Majesty of the Seas after vacation as Shore Excursion Manager to fill in the manger there that was going on vacation.

After getting back on the Majesty of the Seas from vacation, it was fun to be on a ship as manager that I had been an assistant before. It was more work than the Nordic Empress as we did 7 day cruises to 4 ports and the revenue was much higher than on a 3 / 4 day ship. My sales were good and negative comments were low, so life was good, the only thing was, I did not know where I would be going after the 5 weeks on the Majesty. The schedule did not have anything for me after the manager I was covering for came back.

When I was on the Nordic Empress before vacation, my shore side boss had come to me to see how I was doing and had asked me a question regarding the schedule. They asked me what ship I wanted to go to. I told them jokingly, "anywhere out of the Caribbean" as that is where I had worked most of my cruise ship career and was looking to work somewhere else just for a change. Now I was trying to get on the same ship as Becky so I should have said, send me to the Monarch of the Seas, but I knew the manager there did not want to leave that ship as the kickbacks there I heard were the best in the fleet.

So the old saying goes, "Watch what you wish for, it just may come true". And I found that out as the new schedule was sent out and it had me going to the Sun Viking after the Majesty in a few weeks. Now the Sun Viking was our oldest ship (my parents cruised on it back in the 1970's), but it had the best route in the fleet........ASIA. I was set to fly to Hong Kong and join the ship there and I would cruise the coast of China, Vietnam, Thailand, Malaysia and Indonesia. Talk about getting out the Caribbean.

It was adios to the Majesty, home for a week before heading out to the Far East. The week at home was fun as I had promised my family I would come for my week off between ships, but when I had told my Jamaican tour operator I had a week off when I was leaving the Majesty, he said, "Come here and stay mon". They offered me a house on the beach by myself, with a maid, car and chauffer (you never want to drive yourself in Jamaica, trust me) and bartender when I wanted. And this was a large two story house that looked like a 1970's porn movie should be shot there (not that I would know anything about that), but family comes first before private a Jamaican beach houses out of porn movie.

It was a 15 hours flight from Los Angeles to Hong Kong, in coach no less. The only redeeming thing was that on international flights you get free booze, so that helped to pass the time when you are the meat filling in a middle seat sandwich for 15 hours. Landing in Hong Kong I remembered what my shore side boss told me, that there would be someone with a sign with my name on it to take me to the ship. Lesson learned, never expect that, always have a backup plan, one that at that time I did not have. Being somewhat hung over from the long flight, I searched the Hong Kong airport for a sign with my name on it, but there was none to be found, not even one with RCCL on it.

Now the internet was just getting popular and at this time in the mid 1990's, it was mostly with business and the wonderful dialup (slooooooooow). Before going to the airport I was at my mother's work where they had the internet and I was amazed when I could look at the configuration of the 747 aircraft I was going to fly to Hong Kong and where I would be sitting. It would have been better of me to look at a map of Hong Kong to find out where I was going, I regretted that at the moment wondering around the airport.

Having given up on finding the mysterious person who was "supposed" to pick me up and take me to the ship, I exited the airport and got in the line (called a queue) for a taxi. After waiting about 30 minutes, I finally got in a taxi and tried to tell the nice man to take me to the cruise ship terminal. He just looked at me like a deer in headlights and I tried using my hands to describe a ship, but that did not work and I'm sure I looked like an idiot to him. He finally gave me his microphone and I found myself talking to the taxi dispatcher who knew very little English. My attempts at communication were failing miserably and it was the middle of the night, and I was quickly running out of options. Finally I remember I had some photos in my carry on that was in the backseat of the taxi with me. I whipped out a photo of the Costa Classica I had and showed it to the driver who then smiled and started staying something in his particular Chinese dialect and off we went to the Sun Viking.

I should have known, but did not take the time to research, that Hong Kong is actually 3 distinct places, Hong Kong Island, Kowloon, and the New Territories. The cruise ship terminal was in Kowloon, across the water from Hong Kong Island. It was just after midnight when I got to the ship, I was able to sign on and get my cabin and by 12:45AM Hong Kong time, I was in a ship's lounge having a drink with the staff, a few of which I had known from previous ships which always make things easier (unless of course you did not like that person, but that was not the case here). So it was time to settle in and start to enjoy being in Asia which was an eye opening experience to say the least, so let's get to some Asian stories.

Before I knew it I was doing my first Asian tour talk in front of about 300 people on the ship . The Sun Viking did not have TV's in the cabins, just radios, so instead of videotaping my tour talk and putting on TV 24 hours a day, instead it was just my voice on channel 5 on your cabin radio. I had done tour talks in the past where I had not been to the actual port before and would just have to "wing" it. Just as before I had to wing it, but since this was Asia, it would be difficult to pull this off, I had just studies Frommer's guide for the area and up on stage I went telling them all about the beautiful Chinese ports they would be visiting.

After my first tour talk a passenger came up to me and asked how many years I had been working in Asia as she said I really knew the places. First I thought I had been caught and she had been teasing me and calling me out on my ignorance of the area, but after a few minutes I found her to be quite honest and sincere and she really thought I knew the area well. I could have just lied to her, but I could not do that, so I told her the truth, that I had actually not been to these ports yet and she was shocked, but still bought a tour for her and her husband for every port we went to based upon my recommendations and she loved the tours.

One side note to giving tour talks to the passengers in Asia, it was the first time I had to explain to my passengers the difference between a "Western" and "Eastern" style toilet and it was something to pay particular attention to on the tours we went on as some had one style of toilet while others had the other. The difference is a Western toilet is one with a toilet bowl, and you would do your business and flush it afterward and be on your way. The Eastern toilet is basically a hole in the ground, with some track pads on either side of it. You just had to squat over the hole and do your business and then go outside the toilet where hopefully you would find some running water to sanitize your hands with (this was before the days of everyone having a bottle of hand sanitizer with you).

The funniest experience with this was when we did a train ride from Shanghai to Wuxi. When we got on the train in Shanghai, I asked where the restroom was and a nice Chinese lady who worked on the train told me where it was, but that it was not open for use while in the train terminal. I did not think anything about it, but being a person who followed the rules, I waited until the train left the station and then headed to the restroom. Upon entering through the door she told me was the toilet, I quickly understood why it was not open while in the train station, and that was because it was an Eastern style toilet and the train's toilet was just a hole in the bottom of the train (with the usual traction pads on two sides of the hole). So I did my business in a rattily, moving train and thought of how some of our older passengers would be able to handle this. So a notice to people, who have not traveled outside their "comfort zone", be prepared for anything.

Earlier in the book I talked about fog watch, which was a joke we played on new, first time crew members. We were cruising one night off the coast of Indonesia and I was on the fantail (back end of the ship) with some other crew members when I saw on the very back deck, one of our Pilipino quarter masters sitting on a high chair with her hands on a really big spotlight. She was moving it back and forth towards the water at the back of the ship like she was looking for something. I laughed and asked one of my friends if that was the Asia version of fog watch joke and they looked at me seriously and said, "No!" she is on "Pirate watch". I laughed when they said that, but then found out it was no joke. When a ship is traveling in the far reaches of the world, outside the security of a local first world coast guard, a ship must take care of itself from pirates.

The story goes that local pirates would take their small fast boats and come up at the rear of a ship, or along the side and throw grappling hooks over the deck rails and climb up and rob people on the ship, or worse, take over the ship. This is why when I looked over the side of the ship, I saw the spotlights from the bridge wings (the part of the bridge that hangs over the side of the ship) that were pointing backward down the side of the ship at night, they were on the lookout for pirates. I spoke with a bridge officer one day and he told me that they could take care of themselves, but would not tell me exactly what armament they carried beyond the usual pistols that I was told most cruise ships carry. The way he described it, it sounded like the ship had some assault weapons or something like that to fend off any would be pirate trying to raid the ship. For years after leaving Asia, I would read on the news about cruise ships being boarded and even commandeered in places around the world and that always made me think back to pirate watch on the Sun Viking.

One of my most embarrassing moments on ships was not something that I did, but something I watched my fellow countryman do while in Saigon, Vietnam. We were on an all day tour of

Saigon (now Ho Chi Minh City) and we stopped outside the abandoned US Embassy as that was part of the tour. Now being a history buff of sorts, being at the US Embassy in Saigon was a big thing for me as I was thinking of the evacuation of it during the last days of the US Vietnam war. I sat there on the sidewalk outside the compound and closed my eyes to try and imagine the chaos and tragedy that happened those last days of the war. My concentration was disrupted by some loud noises not far from me. I opened my eyes and look over to see some Americans on our tour/ship who were buying trinkets and crap from a local street vendor and I got pissed off as the passengers were not looking at the ex-Embassy of their home country, and seemed to not have cared less about the history that was right in front of them. I guess it is my own fault for expecting the awe of the area from my fellow countrymen, but the scene enforced the idea of "stupid Americans" that was commonly said and I would usually try to defend, but there was no defense at this moment.

Onto a different subject that has nothing to do with Asia or even cruise ships, but I quick story I witnessed over time on the Sun Viking in Asia so I thought I would include it in this section. There once was an extremely hot hot hot, oh, did I say hot dancer on a ship, and a crew staff member that was in love with her. She had a boyfriend back home (wherever that was), and he was single and determined to make her his girlfriend. He was of average looks I guess, shorter than average, but with a nice happy personality which is why he was a cruise staff member. Mostly when you see guys trying to go outside their league so to speak, they do stupid things and end up embarrassing himself. This guy lavished her with kindness, understanding, gifts and attention and the dancer and everyone on the ship knew he wanted to date her.

It took some months, but to all of our surprise, one day in Singapore we saw them holding hands walking down the streets of Clark Quay and I thought, dang, he actually pulled it off. They dated at least until I left the ship some months later and I don't know what happened to them, but the sheer will and constant devotion to an end goal paid off and I never have forgotten how persistence can pay off.

A travel note: One of the greatest places I have been to is the Grand Palace in Bangkok. I describe it as it is worth it to get on a plane wherever in the world you are, travel the countless hours to get there, go spend a day at the Palace, and go back to the airport to go home and the trip would be more than worth it, that should say it all.

Sticking with Bangkok, I had the great fortune to go and spend two days there on a ships tour, it was the first cruise ship tour I had been on that was an overnight tour. During the tour I got to see some great Thai dancing, see elephants walking down a highway and stopping traffic, ride in a tuk tuk (Google that to see what I mean), have a glass of wine at the Orient Hotel overlooking the Chao Phraya River and visit Patpong street at night. I have to stop right there at Patpong street. If you have never heard of it, well, it is one of the strangest places I have been to and let me tell you why. It is a street that hosts bars, brothels and sex shows........yes, sex shows. I hope I have your attention now, so I will continue.

So I was walking down Patpong street with the ship's hostess from North Carolina whom I had been great friends with and all the crew on the ship wanted us to date....wait, what about Becky? Well, as things happen with distance and the such, the short version is that Becky and split up after I got to Asia, I won't bore you with details, but it was sad after our years of being together. So back to the story on Patpong street. So there I am walking down Patpong street with the ship's hostess and we stop by for a drink at an outside bar. We were enjoying our drink when I look out at the woman who appears to be managing the bar we are at and she is giving us the evil eye. I look around and notice that all of the Western men at the bar were sitting with Asian looking woman and it hit me, she was the Madam of the bar and woman I was sitting with, a blonde southern bell was messing with her business in some way or another.

We finished our drinks and headed down the street to check out if there really were sex shows going on or if it was just people pulling our legs, so to speak. After a few minutes we realized that no one was pulling our leg as we went from venue to venue and looked at what they offered in terms of entertainment. Needless to say we were shocked, my hostess friend was much more shocked when we read the menu items of the offerings at the shows. Since this is a PG-13 type of book, I'll try and be discrete, they were all live shows with woman/men/girls/boys and every combination in-between which included props like ping pong balls, darts and glass tables. That is as far as I will go with describing the entertainment of Patpong street, but needless to say I have never since seen any offering like that with the exception of Amsterdam, but Amsterdam was pale in comparison.

My hostess friend and I decided not to go into any of the shows that night, I guess it is bad form to go and see a sex show with someone you are just starting to date, go figure. One of the funniest things though was the menu at these places, I kept trying to buy them from the doorman so I could bring one back to my friends in the states and show them what the bars in Bangkok offered, but no one would sell me one. I told them if they copied them and laminated them I would have paid $20 US dollars for one, but they would just ask in their broken English, "how would I show people what we offer", they just did not get it. Not very entrepreneurial I thought, but who was I to judge. I never did get a menu to bring home dang it.

It was on the Sun Viking that I heard a few of the funniest things I have ever heard a ships Captains say. One of them was at the Captains cocktail party, the Captain was a nice, quiet and somewhat shy grey haired Norwegian man who was always very polite and nice in his shy way, but give him a microphone and his persona changed and he was a showman in a way. Anyway, at the end of this one cocktail party, they were taking questions from the passengers for the Captain, one woman gets the microphone and asked him, "Why do they call a ship a her?" He quickly answered, "Because it takes a man to control her, good night", and he walked off the stage to the laughter and ooooo's and aaaaa's of the passengers, a great moment indeed.

This same Captain one day was making his noon announcement that Captains always do on a sea day and I was walking by the gift shop when I heard the Captain say with his Norwegian accent, "The seas might be a little rough today and you will feel the motion of the ocean. I suggest you take a pill, just make sure you take the right one. And if the motion of the ocean gets to you, lie in bed and hold onto something hard". That kind of stopped me in my tracks as I asked myself if the Captain has just suggested that you lie in bed and hold onto something hard, and yes he did say that, have to love that Captain and his sense of humor, but sometimes they should have just taken the microphone away from him.

One item I got to experience in Asia that I have not been able to get here was actually at McDonalds, yes McDonalds. Actually it was a joke in Asia that we called McDonalds the "American Embassy", as it was a place you could go and feel like you were back in the United States, well, kind of. Anyway, they served something over there in McDonalds that I have never seen here in the United States and it was the best thing I have ever eaten at McDonalds, it was the "Samurai" burger. Basically it was a hamburger with teriyaki sauce on it and it was incredible. It was so good that one time I brought one back to the ship, and the other Shore-Ex person who was a vegan smelled it and then could not take it anymore and she ate my Samurai burger and I had to go back onto the pier again to get my lunch, it was that good.

One final note on working on a cruise ship in Asia and that it was the only place I knew of where, in order to have the ship clear customs and immigration when getting into a port, the gift shop manager had to be up and at the gift shop before the ship could be cleared and the passengers let off the ship. Why you ask would a gift shop manager have anything to do with the coming into port and clearance by local officials of the ship, the answer is simple, because before the ship was cleared, we would have to give (bribe) the officials with cartons of Marlboro cigarettes and bottles of Jack Daniels whiskey, that was just the way it was in Asia although the gift shop manager hated getting up early every port morning to give away his merchandise.

Well my time in Asia ended and it was one of the best contracts I had ever had, but unfortunately I never went back there working on a cruise ship, although I did go to Singapore one time for a long weekend when I lived in Miami, that was a long way to travel for a 3 day weekend, but it was worth it. So where to next you ask? Well, since you asked, the past few months I had been dating the blonde southern bombshell from North Carolina, something that kind of made me laugh that I went all the way to Asia to date a Southern Belle, but once again, go figure. Her next ship was the Monarch of the Seas so of course I was trying to get assigned as Shore-Ex manager there to be with her, which would have been fun since I believe Becky was still there, so that would have been interesting, or scary, but as always when I am trying to get to the Monarch, I was denied.

Instead the company said they needed me in Alaska which was actually a compliment as not many people got to go to Alaska as it was such a busy and profitable route for shore excursions, they only sent those who they thought could handle the fast pace that Alaska tours brought on. So I joined the Legend of the Seas when it was in the Caribbean, just before it went through the Panama Canal, going to Hawaii on its way to Vancouver to home base there for the summer for the Alaska season.

I loved the ship and to this day it is probably my favorite out of all the 17 ships I worked on (next the Radiance class ships I would work on years later). I was on the ship as an assistant Shore-Ex to learn Alaska and the other routes the ship did like the Panama canal. One highlight of my cruise ship career was the "Fam" trip I took to Alaska. On one of our last stops in Hilo Hawaii where the ship would then go to Vancouver to start the Alaska season, I got off and flew to Seattle Washington. You see a Fam trip is a familiarization trip for those who had not been to

Alaska before. Instead of having to wing it like I usually did when going to a new port, they actually sent me there ahead of time so I would know what I was talking about.

So in Seattle I met other Shore-Excursion people from other cruise lines and went on a 5 day fam trip all around South East Alaska. An average day would consist of taking a plane to Juneau, then directly going to a Seaplane to take an aerial tour of the area, then go on a bike tour, then a kayak tour, then back to the airport for a helicopter tour, than back off to a hotel where your bags were waiting for you in your room and then they took you to a great dinner where you just ordered whatever you wanted, money was no object. Needless to say this was one of the best work week/vacations I have ever been on.

Meeting the Legend of the Seas in Vancouver, I boarded my ship for a summer in South East Alaska, one of the greatest places on earth. One interesting thing I noticed as I was walking on the pier to join the ship, was seeing the Cruise Director of the Legend being taken off the ship in a wheelchair. What the hell I thought, I obviously missed something while I was touring around Alaska the past few days. Of course I knew something was up, as this was the cruise the Cruise Director's wife was cruising, which would put a damper on the CD's girlfriend who was a crew staff member and she had to be quiet while his wife was on board. The funny thing is everyone on the ship knew about it, except the wife, that is until this cruise.

So someone tells the wife about the affair, she confronts her husband's mistress, and the next thing you know he is apparently attempting suicide with alcohol and pills, hence being taken off the ship in a wheel chair. We never saw him again, but on a positive note, the assistant Cruise Director was promoted to Cruise Director and she was one of the best Cruise Directors I ever worked with, that was good for us, not so much for the departing CD.

One funny thing that happened on my first contract on the Legend, was a woman came on board with a dog…..Someone shore side had promised her she could bring her dog on as it was a therapy dog to help the woman relax or something like that. Well, that is good and fine, but no one shore side had the thought to tell the ship, probably because the ship would have said noooooo! But they let the woman and her dog on and then came the issue of where would the dog go to the bathroom. So the Captain had a wooden box made about 3 feet by 3 feet and they filled it with the absorbing liquid they used for spills in the engine room, kind of like kitty litter. They put it on the bow and all cruise passenger would walk by and wonder what in the world that was, unless of course they saw the dog taking a crap on one of his walks.

My next ship was the Enchantment of the Seas as the Shore Excursion Manager and I flew to Aruba to meet the ship. It was close to brand new having only been sailing about 3 months. The ship was just starting to settle into its Eastern/Western itinerary which as you know, is my favorite route(s). So let's get started with some stories from the Enchantment, there are some good ones I believe.

During this contract I got to experience something no one apparently every had. Getting hundreds of passengers off an island, but from another port, or lack of port I should say on the other side of the island. It happened like this, I go ashore to load my morning tours in good'ol Grand

Cayman, where eventful things seems to happen to me. It was a rough ride on the tender to shore and the forecast was for it to get even rougher, but the Captain decided to go ahead and stop at the island with the hopes that the forecasted bad weather would not be as bad as they thought, well that did not happen. After getting about 800 passengers off the ship, the Captain suspended tender operations due to the rougher seas. So there we were stuck in Grand Cayman, not a bad place to be stuck I must say. But now it was up to me and my contacts shore side to find out how to round up 800 odd passengers who were all around the island by this time and get them back to the ship.

It was strange to look at and see the Enchantment leaving without me, but there it went, heading north to go to what was going to be our backup tendering area, which was actually the north side of the island and nowhere near any docks. I managed to get just about every tour van on the island to queue up in Georgetown and started getting passengers who seems to line up for miles, up to the North Sound near the golf course up there. After hours and hours, we managed to get what we hoped were all the passengers there and we waited for the tenders to arrive to take us back to the Enchantment. Sounds good I bet, well the ride to the ship was about 45 minutes as we had to go through the North Sound which as not that rough, but then when we went through the channel and out into open water, it as one heck of a wild ride to say the least. Luckily there was a bar near where the tenders were picking people up, and I got to have a nice cold beer after a chaotic morning and afternoon. After getting back on the ship, the Safety Office and cruise staff that were with me on the island headed straight to the Safety Officers cabin to have a drink and de-stress a bit before we went to brief our bosses on what had happened, and there was plenty to tell them.

Later that cruise during the Cruise Directors staff meeting, the CD started talking about all the things that we did wrong on the shore in Grand Cayman and criticizing everything we did, well I could not take that so I stood up interrupting him as he bad mouthed us and I began to tell him that of course this had never been done before in the history of cruising in Grand Cayman (at least not to our knowledge) and that we were stuck in an impossible situation that we had just some control of and were at the mercy of what the island could do and that his staff had done a great job and it was easy for him to Monday morning quarterback us as he was sitting comfortably on the ship while we were in port doing the best we could with the resources we had. He backed down immediately and then started complementing us for our efforts. I looked over at the other staff in the meeting that were on the island with me and they were smiling at me and later thanked me for standing up for them. We weren't looking for praise, but sure as hell did not deserve such criticism.

Sticking with the Cruise Director let me tell you a little bit about him. He was a great CD, fantastic with the passengers, and pretty good with the crew except for the occasional Monday morning quarterbacking I described earlier, oh and he was a sex addict.......what you say, how do I know that, well because he told me. He used to leave me VHS porno tapes and told me to watch them.....excuse me......so I would take them and he would ask me what I thought of them. I then had to go and find people with other tapes to lend to him, it was a game I had to play and I thought it was hilarious. Of course this is the CD that we were told got banned from a hotel in Miami for masturbating on his balcony, lucky for him there are lots of hotels in Miami.

One day he thanked me for putting some passenger on the Kon Tiki tour in St. Thomas, why did he thank me you ask, well it was because he told me he had sex with the guys wife while he was out on the tour and she was incredible in bed (and out of bed as he told me the graphic details). It was somewhat stressful working for that CD, but all in all he was a good CD.

The Legend of the Seas was the first ship I worked with that had email (for only about 10 people on board including the Captain), and since the Enchantment was a new ship, the managers had email on this ship as well. Where am I going with this, well the Chief Purser had been flirting with me for weeks now….wait….what about the hostess I was dating, well back on the Legend I got a "Dear Guy Fax" where she dumped me by fax of all things, I had my payback years later, but that is a story for later in the book.

So the Chief Purser kept asking me when I was going to go to her cabin to watch a movie. I'm not the sharpest crayon in the box, but I figured that was code was something, you be the judge. So she sent me an email asking if I would like to watch a movie in her cabin on a certain night and I accepted. Well the day came for our "date" and I got an email from her saying she could not make it as the Hotel Director had asked her to dinner that night to entertain some high profile passengers on board that cruise. But when she sent me the email, she accidentally copied the Hotel Director and Captain on the email and I saw that and laughed out loud in my back office. The HD was a great older British gentlemen with decades at sea and we got along great. So I go into his office where he is busy working on something and I say to him, "Why are blocking my date tonight?" He stopped what he was doing, took off his glasses, look at me and said, "What are you talking about", then it hit him and he snorts and says "What the hell I am running here, a dating service" and I laughed and walked out of his office to talk to the horrified Chief Purser when I told her she had copied the Captain and HD on her email to me. That was a lesson to her to watch who she sends emails to, but we all had a good laugh at it.

Have you ever wondered what those lines are that hold the ships to the pier when they are in port. The lines are called "Hawsers", and sometime they don't hold the ship to the pier. One time coming into Cozumel when there were high winds, the ship was parallel to the pier, but about

25 feet away from it and the hawser from the bow to the pier was connected. I was standing at the gangway with the ships hatch open and I was watching us attempt to dock. All of a sudden I heard an extremely large noise that sounded like a cannon had going off. I looked out through the hatch and saw a huge plume of water rising towards the bow of the ship around where the hawser from the bow to the pier would have been. As I watched the water explode, I noticed a guy who had been sitting on the huge cleat that the hawser was connect to on the pier running away from the ship. In case you haven't guessed it by now, but the hawser had snapped and luckily for the guy sitting on the cleat on the pier, the line went down to the water, if had gone toward the shore, it would have cut that man in two. I'm sure he went to the bar when he left the pier, as soon as he changed his underwear. Every time I walk on a pier by a ship and see the lines tying the ship to the pier, I wonder which way they would go if the snapped, luckily I was never on a pier when one snapped and I hope to keep it that way.

Another day in Cozumel I actually went scuba diving. Since quitting the dive business, I rarely went scuba diving, but the dive manager on the Enchantment got me to go diving from the beach there at the end of the pier with a couple of dancers that wanted to go. It was a blah dive as the coral is all destroyed from all the tourist there, but it was nice to be underwater. We worked our way farther from the beach until we started to hear some loud noise and figured it was the Holland America ship that was docked next to the Enchantment. Of course you should never go near a ship underwater when they don't know you are below, but when you are bored on a dive, well you know. So we signaled for the two dancers to head back to shore, and the dive manager and I went towards the noise. We saw the dark blue hull of the Holland America ship and we swam up to it and touched its hull and gave a "hang loose" hand signal to each other, it was pretty juvenile I assure you. Then the normal humming sound that the ship was emitting underwater changed to an extremely loud thunk thunk thunk thunk and then we looked at each other will eyes as wide as silver dollars as we simultaneously figured out that the ship was leaving the dock and the sound was the propellers going in reverse to back away from the dock. We were not far from the bow thrusters which we could see and knew if they used them, the water would suck from the port side where we were and we realized we could possible get sucked in.

We both started swimming down fast and away from the ship until we reached a few coral heads and we grabbed on to them, yeah I know you are not supposed to touch the coral, but it was dead long before we touched it. As we held onto the coral, our bodies were being pulled in the direction of the ships propellers, not really strong where we could not keep our hold on the coral, but strong enough to gently pull our legs in that direction. I admit it was not one of the brightest things to do, but what can I say, the boring dive turned into one to remember.

Now the next story is one that was told to me time and time again. I heard it from crew, staff and a Hotel Director or two so I believe I have all the information correct and it is one you probably have not heard about as the cruise line wanted to keep it hush hush as you will soon find out why. It involves one of the most critical events on a ship, the precious Big Bucks BINGO. It was on a ship I did not work on and never worked on, but here is how it went down as told to me by countless people who were there.

There was an assistant Cruise Director on a ship who found a way to rig it so that he would know the winning card. I guess I should let you know the assistance Cruise Director (ACD) is the one in charge of the bingo program on a ship and it is big money. So what this guy did was to pick a card and write down the numbers that would make a winning big bucks bingo for that card, then found some cute young woman and would approach her and say he would give here the winning card and they would split the winning. He would tell here that is the way it was done, and why not, when half of a big bucks bingo could be worth thousands of dollars. So at the final bingo, he would call out all the numbers on that card as he was the one who pulled the numbers so it was easy for him to do it. The young woman would win thousands of dollars and the ACD would keep the other half.

This went on for about 5 months or so until he made one mistake, one of the women he picked was good friends with someone who worked in the shore side office in Miami. When she got back from her cruise (with her winnings), she talked to her friend that she had been the one "picked" to win the big bucks bingo on her cruise. Naturally her friend who worked for RCCL said, "What

what what!!!!!" and notified her boss who called someone and they called someone, you get the picture.

So how did they catch the guy, well they sent in a spy on the next cruise. The spy flirted with the ACD all cruise and did her best to make sure he would pick her as the bingo winner, and she did a good job as he called her on her cabin phone to talk about how it worked. What the ACD did not know was that while he was talking to her on the ships phone, there were many more people listening in on the call, including management on the ship and people in Miami who were listening. After the call the ship's security officer went to the ACD's cabin and I guess you could say arrested him and next thing you know the guy is in the Captains office where he is accused of rigging the big bucks bingo and they showed him the evidence they had.

He did not deny it and told them how long he had been doing it and that he had made about $100,000 on the scam. Here is the funny part, they fired him, no surprise there, but do you think they prosecuted him for it……..NOPE. They did not want the publicity and having people who were on that ship back in the 1990's come to RCCL and demand money for bingo they might have won. So the guy lost his job, but got to keep all the money, and from what I heard, we was wanting to quit anyway. And since they did not want the publicize it, they could not give him a bad recommendation, so you could say he got away with it. That is the only scam I have heard of like that on ships, but I always wondered what other scams were going on that they never found out about, food for thought.

Now for another somewhat embarrassing story about me, cause if you can't laugh at yourself, you can't laugh at anyone, and who doesn't like to laugh at other people. So there I was sitting quietly at my desk on the Enchantment when the theatre manager comes in and asks me if I want to be in the crew show (a show done by the crew for the crew held every now and then in the main lounge at midnight after the passenger shows, they are for crew only). I gave him my usual, no I'm busy response and then he says, "We are doing the Full Monty". For those who don't know, the Full Monty was a movie and the title refers to going nude. He had my interest now as I had never heard of that being done at a crew show, and I ask him, "Is it going to be a real Full Monty", and he smiled and said yes. For the life of me I have no idea why I said the next thing and still don't know to this day, but I said, "Count me in".

Now the bit was supposed to choreographed, with costumes (at least at the beginning), lasers and smoke effects, just like a production show, but it never got organized, we never even met to talk about it, the idea just never happened. Why would I bring up something that never happened, well it was what spawned out of what did not happened, that made this story.

So the day of the crew show came and the dive manager came to me and asked me if I wanted to do a bit in the show with him. He was quite disappointed that the Fully Monty bit did not happen. I told him it was too late, no time to develop a bit, rehearse and all that. He then told me how he came up with a bit and he would take care of everything. After explaining the bit to me, once again for some strange reason I said yes that I would do it, what was I thinking?

The next thing you know it is close to midnight and I am backstage of the main lounge and I can hear all noise from the audience as the crew members were coming into the lounge for the show. Before I go on I have to say that I was stone cold sober at this point, I had not had one drink that night as I wanted to have my wits about me as I performed (if you want to call what I was about to do as "performing"). We were the opening act so at least it would be over soon. On stage were two sets of steel drums, you know the ones that reggae bands have, the inverted drum with the dings in them. Anyway, the time comes for the show, and as I walk on stage just behind the stage left drum, I notice that on the wings of stage right is the Captain, Staff Captain, Hotel Director and others, great I thought. The dive manger walks out from stage right and stands behind his steel drum. They applauded us coming on stage but then quieted down as we just stood there and looked out at the crowd. When it was quiet, the dive manager and I looked at each other and then slowly nodded our heads to each other, then we unhooked our tuxedo jackets, looked at each other, then nodded again, then undid our tuxedo pants and dropped them to the floor around our ankles.

The audience started applauded as we stood there with no expression on either of our faces and wearing matching Royal Caribbean boxers shorts which everyone loved. As the crowd quieted down yet again as we looked straight out with no expressions on our face, we looked again at each other, nodded, then went and pulled our boxer shorts down to join our pants around our ankles. We had nothing else on and were barely being covered by our tuxedo shirts and of course the steel drums that blocked most of the view as they are about the height of our waists. Then the steel drum music started and we both lifted our arms out to our side and lifted them up to the ceiling, lifting up with them our tuxedo shirts.

I wish I could have blamed alcohol for where I was at that moment, but could not. So the steel drum music starts and we start gyrating our hips around like we were playing the steel drum with our tally whackers. This was taken from a bit the dive manager had seen where a guy plays a piano with his Willy, we were just doing it reggae style I guess. Now most of the crew could not see our private parts, except of course for those on the wings of stage right and left, so the Captain and others there had full view of us and what was being flung around on stage. And of course those in the front row who were looking up at us had a direct view of our Willies flying around as they could see under the steel drums. No big deal I thought, they can have their peep show and that would be that, but Nooooooooooo, I glance down and see the ships videographer with her camera pointing right up at our Willies as they flopped around on stage. Crap I thought, now this is on tape. I guess it is lucky video on the internet was not really a thing back then, or else it might have gone worldwide instead of just for the crew of the Enchantment.

Finally the music ends, the dive manger and I pull up our boxers and our pants, then the dive mangers girlfriend comes out on stage, hands us both ice packs that we place against our groin, and she says into the microphone, "Lets here it for the swinging ding-a-ling brothers", and we walk off stage to the thunderous applause of the crew and I was glad it was over, the things we do to entertain our fellow crew members. By the way, the Captains and people on the stage right were laughing out loud during the show, so I felt somewhat safe I still had a job, thank goodness we did not have HR managers back then.

Two items to point out after this story, before the show went on, I joked with the dive manager and said if I don't get a girlfriend after this performance, I never will on this ship. Well that night after the show, I started hanging out with and eventually ended up dating one of the youth staff, so I guess it was worth it. Another item is a week later, I was in the office of the Chief Purser, the one who wanted to watch the movie with me but we never did. We were going over some Shore-Ex financial numbers and she said, "You know the video of the crew show is on the crew channel". I said that I knew about it, but had not seen it and she then proceeds to start describing what she saw on it, I just stopped here and asked, "Did you like what you saw", and she said, "Yes", with a big smile on her face. I told her, "That is all I need to know about the video" and I never did watch it. I did get some cat calls and whistles from some female (and some male) crew members that week as I walked down the hall, how sexist ☺.

One last note on the crew show, a few weeks after I left the Enchantment, they had a crew part on the back crew deck of the ship. During the party the Theatre Manager did a BA to the camera there for the guys on the bridge to see, and he got fired for that. It was a different Captain which was lucky for me, as just weeks before that the new Captain would have seen the ding-a-ling brothers perform, and I'm sure we would not been so well received as the Captain who loved our act.

I guess you could sex is a theme of sorts in the past few pages, so let's keep that going with this story. There was a crew party being held in the crew bar that was being promoted by the gift shop girls. They advertised it as a "Lesbian Party" and you had to be a woman, or be dressed like a woman to attend. Being one to never want to be left out of a party, a few of us asked some of the female dances to set us up for the lesbian part, and set up they did. Just before the party, the girls came down to our cabins and put make up on us, and put us in some dresses they had with them. Now the assistant Cruise Director on the ship and was an actual drag queen and had his own girdle and outfit, the rest of us including the dive manager and Norwegian macho sports directors got fitted for a night with girls.

Before they put the nail polish on me, I said wait, I want some nail polish remover to put in my cabin so when I come home tonight I can take it off and don't have to go work in the morning with nail polish on, so they brought me a bottle, at least I was thinking ahead, or so I thought, more of that to come later. Off to the party we went, and here is what I have to comment on the party, and that is that women are and can be way dirtier than guys. I could not believe how the girls behaved, but loved every minute of it. They were kissing each other, as well as us "drag queens", they were grabbing each other's breasts, they grabbed our balloons we had in our dresses as those were the only breasts of significance we had, and had us grab their breasts, I guess I can say now that I am a lesbian trapped in a man's body.

It was all fun until some of the girls brought their dildo's and vibrators to the party and started putting them close to our faces and other parts, that is when it was time to leave. So I went home to hear once again the cat calls and whistles from down the crew corridor from other crew members who were working and could not go to the party. Back in my cabin, I got undressed and took the nail polish off my nails, much to my satisfaction that I had thought ahead, but then I looked in the mirror at the mound of makeup on my face, lipstick on my lips, eye liner and so on. Crap I thought, how do I get that off, so being a guy, I get in the shower and proceed to scrub my face with a washcloth and good'ol Safeguard soap and I keep scrubbing away and looking in the mirror to see the makeup still there. So I push the washcloth harder against my face in my desperation to remove the makeup which I finally did, of course my face felt like a raw piece of meat when I was done and I could not even touch it. The next morning I told this to the dancer who had "dolled" me up, and she said, "Why didn't you just use lotion, that would have taken it off", you're kidding me I thought, well, lesson learned. The next time I dress in drag, I will need both nail polish remover and some makeup remover.

The next story is not about sex, but rather when I knew I had been in my job long enough to not be shocked by any events. We were in St. Thomas and I had a tour on a snorkel boat going on that afternoon. I was walking to my office, but was waved at by one of the pursers at the guest relations desk, so I walk over to her and say hi, what's up. She then tells me that they just called and said one of our passengers had died on the snorkel boat tour we had that afternoon. I just calmly looked at her and asked, "Do you have a cabin number?"

It did not faze me a bit and I kind of wondered if I was being insensitive or what, but I knew that I just had a job to do and emotions or shock would not help anyone at that point. So I quickly arranged to have the hostess and a female crew staff member pack up the passengers things in their cabin and arrange for emergency disembarkation for the wife of the victim which is not an easy thing to do an hour before you are supposed to leave port and all local officials from customers and immigration had left for home by then. I got it all taken care of and then we met the victim's wife on the pier just minutes before the ship was to depart and she said something I will never forget. She hugged the hostess and cruise staff member that packed their things for her, gave me a hug, and then looked at us and said, "We had a great time" as she tried to cry, but had been crying so long that she nothing came out anymore. Immediately the hostess and crew staff's eyes started to water and I had a tear welling up as well as I was not expecting her to say that, she appeared to be an incredible woman and I said a silent prayer for her and her departed husband.

During my time on the Enchantment I was settling in as I was the permanent Shore Excursion manager for the ship and was set to go on vacation in a few weeks when an email was being sent around to the Shore-Ex managers from our shore side offices about a job in the Miami office with Shore-Ex and they were taking applications from

Shore-Ex managers in the fleet. Now I had no interest at all in working, not to mention to living in Miami again, but looking at it strategically, I thought it best I apply to show I was a "company Guy", so to speak. So I put in my application for the job and thought that was that, but to my surprise, I get an email from my boss shore side, the one who had originally hired me that she was coming into the office that Sunday when the Enchantment would be there to interview me and to meet her in her cubicle.

Crap I thought, what I am going to do, I don't want to leave ships, I really enjoyed my job, working long hours and 9 months straight, the traveling and so on, and if they offer me the job I could not refuse it, so what was a Guy to do. Sunday arrived before I knew it and I walked past the empty cubicles in the Miami office to meet my boss (it was Sunday remember, so no one was in the offices). I brought with me my resume as one does when going to an interview, and she then started telling me about the job and its responsibilities, pay, benefits and kept on going like she was going to offer me the job right then and there which scared the crap out of me. After we talked for some time, she told me she had a hard decision as she told me the job was down to me or the manager on the Legend (we will call her Nancy) whom I worked with when I was on the Legend in Alaska.

I still remember her putting her hands through her hair as she told me how we each brought different things to the job, my managing diving tour experience they wanted, and Nancy had accounting skills they wanted. When I heard her say that the job was between me and Nancy, I smiled on the inside but not on the outside, she had given me my out and she did not even know it yet.

So after we were done talking, I asked her if the interview was over, she said yes, and then I went on to give Nancy a glowing recommendation for the job describing what an asset she would be to the shore side Shore-Ex management team and so forth. My manger just looked at me and when I was done she said, "You are recommending your competition for the job?" I looked at her and said, "I'm not that nice of a Guy, here is a deal for you", and went on to say that if Nancy got the shore side job, then I would like her ship, the Legend of the Seas to be the permanent manager there. When I finished, my boss just smiled at me and I knew it was going to work out the way I wanted.

The next week I went into the office and walked to the Shore-Ex cubicles and looked at their bulletin board to look at the new schedule that had not been emailed out to the fleet yet, and there it was, Nancy being transferred to the shore side offices and Guy going to the Legend of the Seas after my vacation. Normally things don't work out as planned, and even though I did not know that was my plan before my interview, I knew afterward that it was a great plan and I was going to the Legend as the permanent manager.

Back on the Legend, life was good. I settled in the long haul and my cabin reflected it. Since I was going to be on this ship for who knows how long, I brought with me some creature comforts, like bringing flannel sheets with matching bed spread and pillows. Somehow along the way I ended up with 2 fountains in my cabin as well as a collection of about 15 candle holders. Now candles are a BIG no no on ships for the obvious reason of a safety hazard and fire. Nowadays I know I could not get away with it, but while on the Legend I enjoyed a cabin that was kind of like a spa and I loved it. Work was challenging with changing routes as the seasons changed. We would be in the Caribbean during the winter, and then go through the Panama Canal a time or two and do the Mexican Riviera for a few cruises, then off to Hawaii on our way to Alaska for the summer and then head back down south again until we hit the warm waters of the Caribbean. The next few years felt like home on the Legend and it is some of my happiest times in my cruise ship career with great crew members and a great ship, here are some stories from my time on the Legend.

As I mentioned, I decked out my cabin to be incredibly comfortable, and started eating dinner in my cabin more and more. Technically you are not supposed to have food in your cabin, or candles or fountains for that matter, but I found some ways to make it happen. Have you ever cooked Kraft macaroni and cheese in a coffee maker, well I did many times and even though it does not come out quite as good as when done on a stove top, it is the next best thing. Another fine meal is to get a large can of Spaghettios, add some hot sauce of your liking, mix it up and then put it on Ritz crackers, believe it or not, that is a good meal.

I mentioned ships rules a page or two back and now I need to revisit the old rule I talked about in the beginning of the book, the rule of not sleeping with the passengers. By now, hooking up with a passenger was an incredibly bad offense just like it was years ago, but now they really looked for crew members doing that. This is a story of not sleeping with a passenger, but rather how things can be overlooked. So there I am in the main show lounge on the Legend, headed to have some drinks with the Cruise Director and fellow staff members. On the way, an attractive passenger sitting by herself flagged me over and I went to see what she needed. She proceeded to ask me a ton of questions about the shore excursions and she was buying me drink after drink while she enquired about the tours, and then ship life and so on. The next thing I know, she is inviting me to stay with her in Miami and she would take me to a Rolling Stones concert that was coming up. Seriously I thought, I just met her.

Her flirtations continued and I knew it was time to leave, so I faked that my pager went off (yes, we had pagers back then) and said I had to make a call and I had no plans on coming back. So I headed down to the crew bar for a night cap before heading off to bed. At the bar was the Security Officer and we started talking and I told him about the passenger I was just talking to and to my surprise, he tells me, "Why don't you just go sleep with her, just tell me her cabin number and I will make sure the rolling security does not go down her corridor tonight". I thought he was joking, but I had known him for over a year and I knew he was not kidding. I said, "Aren't you the one supposed to be stopping me from sleeping with a passenger", and he just laughed and said, "We all need to have a good time every now and then".

Then my pager really did go off and I went up to call them back. It was the Cruise Director and he was in the lounge I had just been an and he is telling me that there was a passenger looking for me there and that I should come up and take care of her…..Really, is everyone just trying to get me to sleep with this passenger. I said I was done for the night and headed back to my cabin for some peace and quiet. Later in the cruise I found out that the DJ ended up sleeping with that guest, she was obviously on a mission, and in the end, she got what she wanted.

Here is one of my favorite stories on ships, it involves Alaska, the cops, a train, a helicopter and some grumpy old men. We were in Skagway Alaska and one of the most popular tours was the

White Pass Scenic Railway tour and we had two departures when we were in port. I was at a crew life boat drill which I had not been in months as usually I was busy with my tours, but I told the Safety Officer I would show up for at least one drill during my contract. I showed up to the drill to muster my crew as I was the life raft commander for one section and the crew members looked at me and said, "Who are you". About 10 minutes into the drill I get a call on the radio that I am need immediately on the pier so hand off to the assistant commander who is the one who did the drill anyway since I was never there and headed to the pier.

There I was informed by my agent from the railway tour that there had been an emergency and the train had stopped somewhere up the pass. Here is what happened. Two men in their early 70's got into an argument over a window being open, and somehow it turned violent when one pushed the other and he went down and split his head open and was bleeding badly which caused one passenger to panic, so she pulled the emergency cord to stop the train, and stop it did, I was surprised no one got hurt when it stopped so suddenly. The train conductor called for a helicopter, so one of our tour helicopters that usually took passengers flight seeing over glaciers, flew up the mountain and took the man to the hospital.

When the train got back to Skagway, the police were waiting for the man who pushed the other man who had to be air lifted from the train and they took him to jail. Later that day the man in jail complained of heart problem so they took him to the hospital. The injured man was able to make it back on the ship before sailing as they stitched up his head and he was doing fine, the one that had been in jail was in the hospital and of course did not make the ship. The next day we were in Juneau Alaska and I was dispatching my tours in the afternoon when I see 4 Juneau police officers go onto the ship, hmmmmm, wonder what they are doing, but I went about getting my tours off. Half an hour later the police started walking up the gangway with an older man in hand cuffs, what in the world I thought to myself.

I found out later that the man in cuffs was the one who got arrested the day before in Skagway. This morning the man had left the hospital and went to the airport and hopped on a flight to Juneau, then he just walked back on the ship as if nothing had happened. Well when the Skagway police discovered he was missing, they investigated and found he had flown to Juneau, hence the Juneau police. In the end the man was charged with some type of assault, but was allowed to get back on the ship as long as he came back months later for his court date. That would be a pain for the man as he was from Brazil so he would have to fly all the way from Brazil to Alaska for the court date. That story made for along report to the Captain and my shore side office and I just had to laugh at things that can happen on a tour with grumpy old men.

As I said before, ship life was great, the permanent Cruise Director and I were good friends and she was great to work with. There are not many jobs when your boss, whose office is right next to yours will shout out loud in the middle of the day, "I need tequila", to which I would open my desk drawer and pull out a bottle of tequila and walk in with a bottle and two glasses and say, "You rang". Ah, those were the days.

Now I had been on ships for many years by now and the line had expected me to become a Life boat commander. This is someone who is trained in how to lower, load and pilot a life boat and they were usually managers who were commanders. I had gotten out of it as I was always busy while in port and found it impossible to make it to the training, but eventually they made me make the time to get my Life Boat Commanders License (and get my Liberian Seaman's passport as the ship was registered in Liberia).

I showed up on the promenade deck for my first day of training. The bridge officer showed us how to lower the boat to the embarkation deck, then down to the water, unhook and go for a harbor tour and then come alongside the ship and hook back up and raise the lifeboat back up and into its davits. Most of the crewmembers who were being trained had never been around boat, except the ship they were on. Let me pause for a moment and tell you one of my pet peeves, and this when someone would call a cruise ship a "boat". It is not a boat and here is how you can remember the difference, you can put a boat on a ship, but not ship on a boat, or my favorite way of remembering is, a boat is something you go to when your ship is sinking.

The next week we showed up for training and it was a different officer and he asked us all about our boat handling experience. When it came to me I told him about my working on dive boats in California, and in the Bahamas, and that I was a dive boat and sailing captain when I lived in Grand Cayman. So he nominated me to be the life boat captain for that days training. I organized the crew and got the lifeboat down from its davits, down to the embarkation deck, loaded up the rest of the crew, then now being in the driver seat, I lowered the boat to the water, had the other crew unhook us, and then took us for nice scenic boat ride off of Skagway. The officer order me to bring the life boat back in, so I slowly brought the boat up next to the Legend and right under the hooks and we lifted up the side of the ship and eventually got it back into its davits as it was before the training started.

When I climbed down from the davits back to the deck, the officer told me I could go and to show up two months later for the exam. The rest of the crew did training twice a week for two months to learn how to handle a life boat. Two months later it was time for the written exam and practical exam where you lowered a life boat. I had not looked at the study guide they had given us until I was on the way down to take the test. I met the man who was an official for the Liberian government, he was American , but certified by Liberia to administer the exam. I took the test and got the best grade in the class and then headed out to lower the lifeboat for the official. I got elected to be the commander, so we did what we needed to do and lowered the boat, then the harbor tour and then back up on the ship. After it was done, we had all passed and we were all now Liberian Seaman. I also thought that would be a great pickup line in a bar, "Hi there, I'm a Liberian Seaman".

It was getting near the end of a season in Alaska and I was wiped out, the long hours, and hard work had taken a toll on me. I was the highest rated ship in Alaska for Shore-Ex sales numbers and revenue and low negative comments which made it all worth it, I loved my job. Then one day on of my tour operators who handled some fixed plane flight seeing tours told me I needed to check out a new tour they wanted to offer the cruise line, but that I would have to get off the ship for two nights to check it out. No way I told him, Miami would never allow that, then he told me it was already done, that he had cleared it with my bosses in Miami and that on the next cruise I was to get off the ship in Haines, and I would re-join in Ketchikan as he would fly me there in one of his planes. Wow I thought, I had never been off a ship for a night or two during a contract and was really excited.

So the day came and I had my bag and got off the ship and headed for the hotel, a nice meal and few drinks with some tour operators in Haines. The next morning I got up and it was strange not to be on the ship, I actually felted relaxed. I met the tour agent who had arranged for me to get off the ship and told him I was excited to see the new tour. That is when he told me it was all a sham. The whole thing was an excuse for me to get off the ship for a few nights and relax as he thought I was burning out so to speak. There was a tour to check out, but no way was it viable to sell so we went and looked at it, and sure enough, no way I could sell that tour. So we toured around for the morning and in the afternoon I met with another tour agent and we took some of his rifles and pistols and went out shooting in the Alaskan wilderness, a good day to say the least.

Later in the afternoon I met tour operator who had arranged for me to get off the ship at the airport and boarded one of his twin engine planes along with some of his staff and it was time for a "joy ride" of sorts. It was a great flight from Haines to Ketchikan and instead of just going direct, we flew over some glaciers and did some things a normal tour would not do like going slow and low over some glaciers, it was an incredible flight. Arriving in Ketchikan I thanked my tour operator for a great trip and went to the hotel for one last night sleep off the ship.

The next morning I was on the pier with my bag waiting for the ship to get in. There was work to do and I wanted to get to it after my quick refresh the past day. As the ship pulled up to the dock, I saw the Captain on the fly bridge and waved to him and he waved back. Later on I found out that the Hotel Director and Cruise Director got in trouble for not informing the Captain that his Shore Excursion Manager was off the ship for a few nights. Oh well, sorry they got in trouble, but it was a great quick vacation.

Life was good, but after a few years I was thinking it was time to get a real job and maybe live on land. I guess I should have tried for that shore side job when I had the chance, but I was not ready then and felt I was now. The question was, what to do as ships was really the only think I knew well besides Scuba diving, should I go back and be a diver on a Caribbean island, or get that job on a live aboard dive boat in the south Pacific, or maybe leave the big cruise lines and go to work on a smaller (500 passengers max) high end expensive cruise lines.

As I was thinking about it, my next adventure came to me on the 405 freeway in Los Angeles when I was on vacation and my father had picked me up at the airport to go home and that is when he asked me if I wanted to go to work for the family business. He had plans on expanding it and asked if I wanted to be a part of it. It seemed perfect in a way, get off of ships with a job with benefits, so I said yes.

When I got back on the Legend to what was to be my last contract, my boss from Miami, the one who originally hired me came on the ship and asked me where I wanted to go. Since I had the highest rated Shore-Ex program the past few years in Alaska, and the manager of the other RCCL Alaskan ship was leaving, she said I could go to just about any ship I wanted, maybe even Europe, but for Europe you need to speak another language and I have a hard enough time with English. That is when I told her that I was actually quitting and moving back to California which was not what she was expecting to say the least, but she understood. I had been on ships for about 10 years at this point, far longer than most Shore-Ex's to say the least.

It was ironic that on my last contract something dramatic happened on Royal Caribbean ships, they went dry. Yes, prohibition had come to cruise ships and it caused the biggest stir I had ever seen. You were no longer going to be allowed to drink alcohol except for a Norwegian beer that was like ¼ the strength of a regular beer and tasted like horse piss (not that I know what horse piss tastes like, but it would not be worse than that crap), no hard alcohol at all to be consumed by the crew. I was convinced it was because someone shore side was getting a kick back from the Norwegian beer company, or the company that supplied the beer and they had convinced the cruise line they should go dry. I guess the reason did not matter, but crew parties would not be as much fun anymore to say the least.

I was pretty lucky to be on the Legend that last contract and during prohibition. Some of the ships based out of Miami was using a breathalyzer on the crew when they came back on the ship from their time off in port and many crew were being fired and many quit their jobs because that was the last straw of taking away their freedom (or they were just alcoholics who could not handle being without booze). Why was I lucky, it was because the ship was quite lenient on the whole prohibition thing. Since we were far away from Miami and the corporate offices, rules were not as stringent.

One day in Aruba I was walking back to the ship with a bottle of Captain Morgan's Rum in a shopping bag and who do I run into, the Captain of the Legend. He stops me to talk about work and how things are going, all the while I am sweating as I have a bottle of rum in my bag. Finally the conversation was coming to an end and I thought he would just say goodbye and leave, but instead he bent down, tapped my bottle of rum in the bag and said, "Enjoy your drink" and he walked away.

Of course this is the same Captain I had Christmas dinner with and we toasted the evening with a glass of water. At the end of the dinner, the Captain asked if we needed any booze for the night, but the Casino Manager said he had plenty of booze and the party would start in his cabin at 1:00AM.

Being one to want to follow the rules, I would go to the bar in a lounge and order a bottle of that Norwegian horse piss, but the bartender would pour me glass of Miller Light and charge my card for the horse piss, so it was not so bad in prohibition, at least on the Legend.

Our regular Cruise Director was on vacation and we had a guy who was filling in. We were in our back office and he was complaining because he wanted to throw a party in his cabin for the crew staff and he thought it was silly he could not have any beer, he kept on complaining until I just went into his office and said, "How many cases do you want", he said 8 cases to which I said it would cost him12 cases and he said sure, but how? I then went to my office and got on the satellite phone and called my agent in Acapulco and said I needed 12 cases of Corona on the pier covered with a tarp waiting for us on the pier when we got there in a few days.

We arrived in Acapulco, and I got one of the stage staff guys to get a cart and follow me onto the pier. Out of the way and covered with a tarp in the shade was 12 cases of Mexico's finest beer (ok, not finest, but it was beer). We loaded up the cart with the beer and headed to the gangway where the Pilipino security guard on the ship just waved us through security without checking what was under the tarp. Our first stop was the Safety Officer and Security Officer's cabin where I dropped off one case each in their cabin. Then to my cabin to drop off my two cases, and then to the Cruise Directors cabin to drop off the remaining 8 cases. Why did I drop off a case at the Safety and Security Officers' cabin, well if you are going to sneak beer onto a ship, the least you can do is pay off the people in charge of making sure you don't smuggle beer on the ship.

This story is one of the greatest in my travels, and it happened on one of my last cruises. I was reading the daily log from the Pursers desk which logs all events that happen with the passengers on the cruise. In there they had an entry for a complaint by a man who wanted the tip back that he had given his cabin attendant the night before on the last night of the cruise. Now you may think the man was cheap or wanted to cheat the hard working cabin steward out of his tip, but that was not the case. What happened was that the man found out that morning that his wife had been having sex with cabin attendant all cruise long. The man was not mad about his wife sleeping with him and did not want the cabin attendant fired or anything like that, he just wanted his tip money back as he believe his wife had tipped the cabin attendant enough all cruise long, you have to love ships.

My time on ships was over, so I thought. When I left the Legend, the Captain wished me good luck, but said he wished I would come back to them soon. At the time I thought there was no way that was going to happened, but you never know where life is going to lead you, or lead you back to.

I signed off the ship in San Diego with a mountain of luggage with the things I had collected over the past few years on the Legend, including my two fountains, candle holders and my purple lava lamp. Since this book is about cruise ships, I won't bore you too much with my shore side time for the next few years except to say I went to work for the family business, got married, left the family business to move back to Miami and try and find a job there. I had fallen in love with computers and databases especially when I was working at the family business and had gone back to school to get a degree in IT and had got some technical certifications. We were in Miami and I was looking for a job without much success, but then I saw an ad for a database person for Royal Caribbean in the port of Miami, I applied for the job but did not hear back from them so I called an old friend from my ship days who worked in the Miami office and told her I had applied for a job.

That same day I get a call from the person, who was hiring the position, and I had an interview the next day where he offered me the position and there you have it, I was back in the cruise ship business but this time I was in the dreaded Miami office. It was great to see old friends whom I had worked with, some who now worked in the office and some who were still on ships, but visiting the office. I loved my job and learned a ton about the IT world and databases and I actually enjoyed living in South Florida.

The marriage was not going so good. My wife at the time was working in Manhattan and we had a place there and one in Miami where I lived. So most weekends I would leave work on Friday and go to the airport and fly to New York for the weekend and fly back on Sunday night so I could be back in the Miami office first thing Monday morning. I did this for more than a year until the logistics just got to be too much, so I made a big decision, I decided I was going to leave my great job in Miami and move to Manhattan. My boss was shocked when I told him I was leaving, but he understood why. So I packed up the house and I moved to Manhattan where we had a nice place on the West side with a view of the Hudson river and New Jersey (ok, that was not the greatest view).

I tried to get a job and settle into a New York state of mind, but neither of those were working out for me. They say if you can make it in New York you can make it anywhere, well I found out I cannot make it anywhere and I had to come up with a plan to get a job and get back on track. Then I came up with a wild idea to go back to ships for a while as an IT officer to help get some more IT experience for my resume and then come back to New York. My wife thought it was a good idea, but deep down, we really knew what my going back to ships meant, which I will get to later.

Now getting a job with Royal Caribbean as an IT guy I thought would be easy as I exceeded the requirements of the job description, and I had a decade of cruise ship experience, how many people can say that I thought. My assumption was dead wrong as I applied for the job, did not hear back from them, and when I called, they said that because I used to work for Royal Caribbean, and they would have to do a check to see if I was eligible to work for RCCL after they had reviewed my employment records which would take up to 9 months. What the hell I thought, I would have had an easier time getting the job if I had not worked for RCCL.

I knew there had to be another way, so I came up with a plan, it had its risks, but it was the only viable plan I could come up with. So I called up a person in the Miami office who I had worked for on a few ships. He was the shore side manager for the ships for Shore Excursions. I told him I was trying to get a job on RCCL as an IT officer, but told him about how they have to go through a review process that would take months. I offered to him that if he needed someone to fill in for Shore-Ex or something, that I would be willing to come back, but told him that I would be trying to get a job with IT on the ships. He said he would see, and I had no idea if I would ever hear from him again.

Two days later he called me up and said he needed me on the Explorer of the Seas in two weeks. He had a manger coming back from vacation at that time and no assistant who had any experience. It is amazing how the red tape can be cut when you try and you get lucky. So after a quick trip to Philadelphia to get a physical from a Norwegian doctor I was off to Miami and back to ships, not in the position I wanted, but at least I would be back in the company and hoping I could pull off a miracle.

Life on the Explorer was a far cry from my time on the Legend, I was an assistant Shore-Ex which I did not mind, I was on one of the largest ship in the world at that time, I was sharing a tiny cabin with nice fellow from a South American country who was a musician in a band on board and did not speak any English. As luck would have it, the IT manager on the Explorer was my old friend who was the IT manager on the Legend whom I worked with for years. He was engaged to bridge officer (yes they started having female bridge officers). It was another week before he and his fiancé got back to the ship, so he let me stay in her cabin up by the bridge for a week, which did not go over so well as to why an assistant Shore Ex was staying in a cabin next to the Chief Engineer, but at least it was a week I did not have to share a cabin.

When the IT manager got back, he interviewed me for the job as assistant Systems Manager. The interview consisted of me, him and his assistants asking me questions in the computer room while he pointed a nerf gun at me. I managed to answer most of his questions so did not get shot with nerf bullets too much. After the interview it was a waiting game to see if my gamble of coming back on ships as an assistant Shore-Ex was going to pay off.

It only took a few days before I got the word that I was needed immediately on the Radiance of the Seas as assistant Systems Manager, my gamble paid off in spades as not only was I going to work in IT for RCCL on ships, I was going to one of the newest ships in the fleet and that ship went to Alaska, win – win – win. I called the Shore-Ex shore side manager and thanked him for bringing me back and that I had got a job in Information Systems. He held me to the two week notice I had promised him so they could replace me on the Explorer and before you know it I was off to the Radiance which was based out of Miami at the time.

Time for an IT story, one that was told to me by my friend who interviewed me for the IT job. It appears that while I was off ships and living in California, there had been a mutiny of sorts on ship. Mutiny you say, yes a kind of mutiny, but it was not on the Bounty, but on Royal Caribbean ships. You see, the IT guys on ships were woefully underpaid at the time and they worked day and night and were really one of the most important people on the ship as when they added so much technology to ships, they became reliant on them and the people who administered them..

One simple task that the IT manager had to do was to send the manifest as soon as the ship set sailed. This was a requirement and the ship would be fined if the updated manifest was not sent to US official's (Big Brother). With the easier means of communication, like cell phones and email, it was easier for the IT managers to talk with each other and eventually they came up with a plan. On one set day, all of the IT managers went ashore (for all the ships that were in port that day) and they did not come back. They had called the ship to say they were not coming back on board until pay and conditions changes. The IT manager who told me said he was standing on the pier, right next to the gangway as the Captain threatened him to get back on the ship.

So the ships that were in port could not leave port as no one besides the IT manager knew how to send the manifest so the ships were stuck, and that costs money and upset passengers, you get the idea. It went all the way up to the CEO of Royal Caribbean who got called at home about the mutiny and he was pissed, but in the end, he gave in and agreed to the additional pay and other demands, and then the managers boarded their ships which could then leave port and the manifests was sent.

Now there were repercussions from the mutiny, they got their pay but they lost a stripe and were somewhat demoted, at least for a time. After that the ship realized how much they needed IT people on ships and that having one IT on each ship was not enough, both for the work that had to be done, and for the backup in case something happened to the IT manager so that is why they started hiring assistant IT officers, especially on the bigger ships. The Radiance of the Seas consisted of the IT Manager who had the title of IT Operations Manager and had one of the largest crew cabins on the ship. It actually had a living room and a separate bedroom. There were also 3 assistant Systems Manager, of which I would be one of them.

As good as it was to be on the Radiance and to be an Officer finally, the Radiance happened to the one ship in the fleet where officers did not wear an officer's uniform, instead, everyone wore polo shirts. The ship was low on the polo shirt uniforms so all I had was one that was at least 2 sizes too small, I looked ridiculous to say the least. Then we petitioned to go back to wearing officer's uniform with epilates and stripes on our shoulders. They finally agreed that the polo shirt uniform experiment was a complete failure and the next thing you know, I am walking down the ships hall with my white officer's shirt with epilates and 2 stripes on my shoulder. It was very interesting the first morning I walked down the I95 (the main crew hallway on the ship) with my stripes. I had passed through this hallway for weeks and no crew hardly looked at me or even said hello, now as I walked with my stripes on my shoulder, and most of the crew said, "Good morning sir". I was the same person doing the same job, but now with my costume on, the way I was treated was entirely different.

I thought that being in IT, things would be very professional with the all responsibilities of running the computer systems for a floating city, but the IT guys were more like the divers I worked with over a decade ago. When I met the IT Manager on Radiance, it was at sail away which was a ritual of his as he liked to have his drinks as we sailed out of port after a very long day doing embarkation and the ton of things that needed to be done to get thousands of passengers off the ship, and then thousands back on, all in the same day. I went up to him and introduced myself and he looked at me and said, "I wish you were cuter". That was not the response I was expecting and I said, "Lucky for me I guess". Yes my manager was gay, not just gay, he was Big Gay Al gay and he was very intelligent with IT.

We worked hard and we played hard (sound like my diver days). My boss would always be getting us to have drinks at the end of the day, which was fine by me, but sometimes you really don't want to and should not have a few drinks. One day during sail away, we had an issue with one of the computer systems on the ship. We were waiting for a tech from Miami to contact us via satellite to help us fix the issue. It was sail away time and we were ordered up to the bar above the pool where we usually were at sail away. I was finishing my third long island ice tea that was being bought for me by my manager when the call came in to fix the issue which happened to be with one of our Unix systems.

My boss tells me to go and take the call and fix the problem. I tell him I just had three long islands in a short time and should not by typing command line Unix on one of the ships most critical systems. He laughed and said to get my ass down to the computer room and get it done. I did get it done, although it was not much fun typing command line with one eye shut as I was seeing two cursors on the screen instead of one. My manager was calling me on the DECT phone (the ships cell phone) and giving me encouragement and that he knew I could do it, while he was laughing in-between encouragements. The next cruise the same thing happened and there was an issue, but this time one of the other assistants had to take care of it after their rounds of drinks and I got to watch sail away and laugh on the phone as the other assistant tried to fix the problem while he was half drunk (or mostly, that term is suggestive).

One of the items I used to take care of was disk space on the ships computer servers, as we were always running out of it with all the crap the computer users on the ship put on them. I'm not talking work stuff, I'm talking music, videos, personal stuff and the like. I would get calls about some ones computer not working and I would go and try and fix it only to find they had put all this garbage on their computer, but one funny things was, I could always tell the sexual orientation of a person by looking at their temp internet files (which I needed to do to fix the problem). Whatever porn sites they were going to pretty much told you what team they played for or where their perversions lye.

You would think the IT people would be good at keeping things off the public drives on the ships systems, but one time, one of the assistants forgot I guess. I was looking at space and told one of the assistants he had too much crap on his assigned folder and he said he had not been putting stuff there. I went in and opened up a huge video file that was on his drive and there on a large computer monitor in our computer room is the old assistant who was on vacation and in the video he was having sex with his girlfriend. We all laughed our butts off and knew we had to torment him when he came back. So the first night he got back on board, we were all in the computer room and we started playing his home made amateur porn movie and he turned three shades of red as he could not believe we did not delete it. We told him he was lucky we did not send it all over the fleet, and it was a lesson for him to keep his personal stuff off the public folders, a mistake he never did again.

Being an IT guy on ships was very different than being a Shore-Ex or diver, for one I had a master key that opened up any electronic door on the ship, every cabin, every access, pretty much everywhere, even the bridge. No more knocking on the door to the bridge to see if they would let me in, now I could just swipe my card and enter whenever I wanted to, and sometimes I would go up there for an afternoon tea and snacks as they always had them in the afternoon and the view from the bridge is always an incredible view, so high up and looking forward high above the helicopter pad.

We also got invited to most of the parties that were held on the ship, especially those held by the Safety or Security officer. One night I went to the Security officer's cabin for a party and as I entered, I notice that the entire carpet in the cabin was covered with plastic. I looked at him and asked, "Are we expecting a crime scene tonight?" He said the cleaners always got upset when they would have to come and clean his carpet the morning after one of his parties, so they were proactive this time and covered it with plastic to cut down on the post party cleaning.

That same night something funny happened, at least funny and ironic to me. It was past midnight and the party had been going on for some time and everyone including the British Security Officer was very happy when he got a call on his DECT phone. He gets up to leave and I ask him where he is going. He says he has to go and give a breathalyzer to a crew member. I laughed and said, "But you ware probably drunker than he is", to which he just laughed and went out the door and we continued on without him. An hour later he comes back to his party, grabs a beer and chugs it down. "How did it go I asked", to which the Security Officer responded, "He is being fired", and we just went on with the party, that was ship life after all.

One of the responsibilities of IT was to manager the ships system which took photos of all the passengers and crew for their cards. Now the passengers did not have a photo on their boarding card, but they did get their photo taken when they boarded the ship which was associated with their boarding card, that way, when the guest would come back on board and swipe their boarding card, their photo would pop up on the screen and the security guard could confirm they were indeed the person using the card, a far advance of my first ship where the passengers boarding card was hand written.

Having access to all of the photos was fun for some IT guys, including one of my managers (not the gay one), who would look through the photos at the start of every cruise to check out the new female crew members. I guess you could say it was a one way online dating site of sorts, but it went in line with what people would say about IT on the ship, and that was we knew "everything" and most of the time we did. We would know who was going to be fired so we could lock out their computer accounts the day they were fired, we knew when there were issues with the ship that most of the crew might not know. We all had a second office in our cabins where we had full access to the ships systems as we worked day and night, no matter what time it was, we were always on call. So we used to joke that we could shut down the ships engines from our cabins, and we probably could as pretty much as we had access to all the computer servers on the ship, and just about all of them we had remote access to.

Sometimes I think we would get to know too much. One day the Captain calls me and asked me if I would check a document he had for spelling and grammar and to make sure it was professional. I thought he was kidding, but he said he would like me to look at it and make any changes before sending shore side to the Miami office. I looked over his shoulder at the document and immediately knew what the file was, it was the review of all the officers on the ship under his command. I said to the Captain, "You know I will have to read this to proof it", to which he said he knew. He asked if I needed it on thumb drive and I told him I had full access to all his files and I could review it from my office.

So down to the computer room I go and navigate my way to the Captains computer files, find the one he asked me to review and went ahead and read the document and made the appropriate changes I felt to make it a professional looking document. I got to read about all the discipline that was given to the ships officer, even a few written warning against the Staff Captain that no one knew about. It was nice that the Captain trusted me enough to read through it and one more confirmation that IT does have the keys to the castle, even to the kings room if you know what I mean.

I was learning more than I could have ever imagines about computer systems. Usually in a job you are exposed to just a small segment of an IT infrastructure, maybe just an email system, or databases, but rarely the whole system. The ship had 40 computer servers and over 180 applications and they were all on about every computer language and technology you could imagine. From Unix, to Windows to Linux and Oracle, SQL Server, MySQL databases and everything in-between.

On one of my first days on ships, I was told to go and fix the ship satellite system. I told them I did not know how to which they said that was my problem and that the azimuth probably needed adjusting. They just said to turn off the juice to the satellite dish as if I had to climb into the dome that encased the dish or the emissions it was giving off make it be permanent birth control for me as it would probably fry my boys and make me sterile. Now when someone tells you that, you listen. I went up and applied some critical thinking and common sense and somehow was able to get the satellite feed back up and reconnecting the ship to the rest of the world.

As my work was great, my personal life was not so great. I won't bore you with the details, but the inevitability that we knew would happen with my going back on ships finally happened, and with some irony I believe. You see when I first met to be wife in California, we met in an online dating site, and when we each agreed to a divorce, it was done using instant messenger from my cabin while off somewhere at sea. So we met online, and divorced online, how very modern I thought.

So now I was back to being single again and on ships. I had no idea where my life was going, except for where I was at the moment, and I was in Alaska which always brought a smile to my face. Sometime after being divorced, I was in the mess having lunch with my boss when all of a sudden, one of the most beautiful women in the world walked in; at least I thought she was. My boss looked at her and said something about how hot she was. I agreed with his observations but knew she was out of my league. When we got back to the computer room, my boss already had a search going to find this new gorgeous crew member and it did not take long to find her in the database.

Her name was Daphne and she was a French Canadian from Quebec Canada and was a massage therapist. I really did not think much more about her, as I said before, she was way above my league. Then one night at a Canada day party in the crew bar, I got to talk with Daphne as we ended up sitting at the same table in the bar. The music was as loud as usual so we had to be close to hear each other. I had put my arm around her to bring her in closer to tell her something and we had a great conversation. Now by this time, I did not stay up late at night, so it was time for me to go home after a nice chat with Daphne and in the morning I woke up and remembered I had put my arm around her and thought, oh no, she thinks I am a pervert.

The next day I saw her in the hallway and we talked for a minute and I apologized for putting my arm around her the night before and she just laughed and said she had not taken any offense by it. A few cruises went by and I saw her every now and then, and she was always stunning and incredible. Then one night the IT boys went out for a night on the town or ship at least. We had dinner in the passenger dining room, then ended up in the ships disco for some cocktails and there I saw Daphne in the disco all dressed up in her flowing red dress, she looked like a Disney princess in a way, but a whole lot sexier.

We ended up talking and then found our way onto the dance floor. Now let me tell you I am no dancer. I can pull of the "lawn sprinkler" like any no rhythm white can do, but I was trying to impress her, so with the best of my abilities, which was not much, I danced with her and then thought it would be good if I spun her around like I had seen so many time before (but those people could actually dance), so I attempted to spin her and ended up sending her tumbling down onto the dance floor with her red dress flying in the air. Oh no I thought, but she just got up and laughed and asked me not to do that again.

It was not long after that magical night that we started dating and life was great. I loved my job and I was in a relationship with a wonderful woman whom I could never spend enough time with. The summer was great in Alaska as Daphne loved to do hiking and adventurous things in port. You see I rarely got off in port before meeting Daphne, I could go 3 weeks without ever stepping foot on land as I was always busy with work and I had been to these ports so many times before. But she got me to take some time off and go out and explore and it was great and I was having the time of my life.

Let me divert course here for just a moment and tell you how Daphne got her job on cruise ships. She was in her 20's and living in Quebec Canada as she had lived her whole life. She decided she wanted to go and out and see the world and what a better way to do that than on cruise ships she thought. The past few years she had been working as a massage therapist in Quebec, so she sent her resume out to some cruise lines. Now what Daphne did not know was that the cruise lines did not hire spa people, that part of the ship's crew was handled by a concession company known as Steiner.

It was like my first few jobs on ships, with one big difference and that is that Steiner had contracts with every major cruise line and was on almost every large cruise ship in the world. The cruise lines had forwarded her resume onto Steiner who called her to interview with them in Montreal. Now Daphne had just started learning English not long before and she said that the interview was a struggle to say the least. One day Daphne got the call that she had been hired and that she was to fly to London England for 2 weeks of training. To most that would sound like a dream come true and it was her, but when she tells the story it is one of being incredibly nervous and downright scarred. She had never been outside of Canada (French Canadian Canada to be specific) except for a trip to Cuba she took with one of her girlfriends. She paints the picture of a French speaking Canadian landing in London and barely speaking English. Standing with all her luggage in the "Tube" with her French / English dictionary and relying on the help of strangers to guide her to where her training was.

After her training she went to the Voyager of the Seas which was sailing the Caribbean at the time. During her first contract she mastered the

English language enough that she felt comfortable in her job and living on ship in an English speaking world. After her first contract, she was scheduled to go to the Brilliance of the Seas, but as fate would have it, at the last minute they changed her to go to the Radiance of the Seas which of course was where I was. That one little change in assignments ending up changing mine and Daphne's whole life. Ok, back to the stories.

Her parents came on a cruise when we were in the Caribbean which is always interesting meeting the parents of the woman you are dating. With Daphne it was even more interesting, as her parents did not speak English. As I mentioned before, Daphne was from Quebec and she herself had just learned English a few years before when she was trying get a job on a cruise ship. So she was in her later 20' when she learned English and her parents did not speak any English at all. By the way, I don't speak French even after years of it in school, but I had bought a French English translation book, so I thought I would all set.

The day of their cruise I went to the pier to find them, Daphne could not get off the ship yet as the normal crew was not cleared yet, but my being an IT officer on the ship gave me the freedom to come and go from the ship to the pier when I want as I had to setup and maintain all the computers used on the pier for embarking the passengers. I had seen photos of them and they had seen photos of me, so when we saw each other, out by the taxi stand, and I went to get them and they gave me a big hug and kiss on each cheek, how very French I thought. I could not understand a word they said, but luckily soon afterward, Daphne showed up and she was all excited as where her parents and they spoke to each other so fast there was no way I could even pick up one word of the French they were speaking.

We headed upstairs to get them on the ship and through security. I saw the metal detector and a long line waiting to go through it. I asked the security person if that was the right line and he asked, "Are they with you sir". Now remember, I was wearing my officer's uniform with my stripes on. I told the man yes they were and he then stopped the line and waved us to go through security right then and there in front of the hundreds of passengers waiting in line. I had no intention on "cutting" in line, but since it was offered, I just followed the man. My girlfriend's parents were impressed indeed and yet I had not intended for that to happen, but it goes to show that life on ships with better with stripes on your shoulder, than without.

During out time on the Radiance, I had gone on vacation and Daphne had gone on vacation and we both knew that life was better when we were together than when we were apart. We both wanted to do one more contract, and since she was scheduled to be on the Brilliance of the Seas which was doing the Mediterranean which neither of us had ever been to and what a great last ship and route to be on. Yes I said the last as we both decided that it was time to leave ships and the ocean and make a "real" life for ourselves, but first the Med.

It was not easy to get myself on work on the Brilliance, but with some luck and some perseverance (and a little bit of my threating to quit), I was going with Daphne on the Brilliance. We left from the port of Miami and sailed across the big blue wet thing (the Atlantic) and spent the entire summer and into the fall in the Med exploring ports and seeing things that amazed us. Here are a few stories from out time on the

Brilliance in the Med, one of them you may already know about and seen on TV, we will get to that one.

One of the most different cruises I ever worked on was the Atlantis Charter cruise in the Med. The Atlantis Charter is a gay travel agency that would charter and entire ship for a cruise and then would sell that cruise to their gay cliental. It consisted of about 98% gay men and the rest were lesbians who I guess liked to go on vacation with gay men. They went all out on the charter, I had to install two extra bars (and the computer systems to go with them) by the pool as the Atlantis charter usually broke records when it came to alcohol sales. They even had to order triple the amount of vodka and red bull for the cruise, and even then they had to restock mid cruise. All the bathrooms on the ship were used by men, so Daphne had the experience of going into the ladies room and seeing a bunch of guys in there. She had been on an Atlantis cruise during her time Radiance when I was on vacation, so she knew what to expect.

Now since this is a PG-13 type of book, I cannot tell you all the things that happened on that cruise, but I will say it was one of the funest cruises I have been on as everyone just wanted to have a good time, very little complaining and they just wanted to have a good time, we just needed to turn a blind eye to where they did like to have sex on the golf course, in the spa, the pool the jacuzzi, pretty much everywhere on the ship. Cabin attendants had to get used to cleaning the rooms in the afternoon as most of the passengers did not get up before lunch as they would be out until the sun came up.

I remember one morning I was doing the computer resets at 5:00AM where I would stop one business day on the computer to start another. Usually there was no activity for sales going on at that time, but that morning, I was looking up at the screen and it was like the Matrix with all the bar sales going on around the ship even at 5:00AM.

On the first night of the Atlantis cruise, we were up at our usual sail away and the IT guys and some Spa people were having a drink and watching the boys sail away from Barcelona. We were chatting with a couple who were very funny and wanted to hear about our life on ships. That was all good and fun until one of them took his cabin card and started to "pretend" to swipe it down the crack of my ass, (he never actually touched me) and say "Control Alt Delete" time and time again. What can I say, I was speechless and then my boss was laughing hysterically saying it was the first time he had seen Guy speechless. Daphne was working but it was not long before she found out some gay guys were flirting with her man. The cruise was great and on one of the last nights they had the "White Party" which was the biggest parties of the cruise. Daphne and I were just going back to our cabin after experiencing the White Party when I saw the "Control Alt Delete" boys and pointed them out to Daphne who had heard the story from many of the Spa people. She then leaves me and goes right up to them and says, "Leave my man alone", I was mortified, it was all in joke and the guys did not offend me. The next thing you know the boys and Daphne are hugging each and I am standing there going what in the world is going on. Come to find out, the "Control Alt Delete" boys were also on the Radiance Atlantis cruise the Daphne had worked and they had hung out together.

The boys told Daphne what a good sport I was and that she had a good man and we could come and visit them anytime we like in San Diego where they lived. It was a funny end to a funny cruise and was way better than the lesbian cruise I had been on so many years ago.

The next story is the one you may already know about, but here you will hear it from mine and Daphne's view of working on the ship when the incident happened and we will call it "Over board George". We were sailing in the Med and one morning we came into the port of Kusadasi. Daphne said I need a massage that morning so I went to her massage room and she gave me a seaweed wrap and full body massage, not a bad way to start the day I have to say. As I was leaving her room, I noticed the Hotel Director and other senior officers talking to a woman in the relaxation area of the ship. Daphne had an appointment in a little while so I just left and went to the computer room to get to work. There I found out that there was a big commotion on around the ship and that someone had fallen over board.

The only surprise I thought was that I had gone so many years on ships without anyone falling over board on a ship I was working at the time. Since many years before they started making most of the outside cabins have balconies I thought people would be falling over board left and right due to alcohol or carelessness. We heard that there was blood on top of the canopy that was above the life boats and of course we had to go and look. We went out to one of the upper decks and looked over the side and sure enough, a portion of the canopy was covered in blood. I am not CSI expert, but from my layman's view, I could see what look like a smear of blood trail going down the side of the ship, like someone's hands were trying grab on, but on that smooth canopy, there would be no way for someone to get traction to pull themselves up onto the canopy as they were slick with no handles or anything to hold onto.

Then there was a surprise, we found out the guy's name and that is when Daphne told us that it was the guy who had an appointment with her after I had my massage and that he had not shown up. Looks like he had a good reason not to show up for his massage as he was apparently not on the ship anymore. We were wondering if the ship would actually sail that night as the Turkish police were on board doing an investigation.

What I believe would happen did, we left port and they had a Pilipino deck hand go out on the canopy (with a safety line on) and pressure washed the blood until the canopy was as clean as can be. You see, if we would have been in a US port like St. Thomas or Key West, the ship never would have sailed as the FBI and who knows what other authorities would come on board and do an actual investigation. This was Turkey, and why in the world would they spend time and money investigating a US citizen's death apparently off their coast. The only thing I think they would been mad about was that a US body was polluting their ocean, what real incentive did they have to really investigation as it had nothing to do with Turkey or any of its citizens.

Then there was the Russian angle with the Russian boys that had partied with the honeymoon couple all cruise before the new husband apparently went overboard. The Russians were mysteriously kicked off the ship when we were in Naples and I soon found out why. We were told by a very good source that they had some parties with a woman unrelated to the honeymoon couple. That girl was an 18 years old and she had gone to the nurse to say that her private parts hurt, she then told the nurse that she had had sex with 7 boys in the past few days and nurse told her that her privates would hurt too if she had group sex with 7 men. The girl said it was all consensual and that she wanted to have sex with them at first. But later encounters were not as consensual and it came down to a, they said she said. Although there was a video tape of one of the first group sex encounters with the Russians and the girl that a few people on the ship who watched the video said it looked very consensual to them. I had not and have never seen the tape, so I can only comment on what the people who saw the tape said.

For weeks after that we had to do data queries to give the FBI information on what the honeymoon couple bought, like in the bars, and also the Russians. The poor Captain did not sleep for weeks as he had to deal with the aftermath of the investigation which did not prove much of anything. The new bride was found apparently in the hallway the evening her husband disappeared. She was passed out drunk and security guard brought her back to her cabin, but just dropped her off at the door as she awoke and went it. The had been partying like it was 1999 all cruise and most of the crew that saw them did not think they were like other honeymoon couples as they spent a lot of time apart and partying with other people.

There was a lawsuit that was filed against Royal Caribbean that I thought had no merit, I mean it came down to drunk and stupid. Someone was drunk and someone did something stupid, people do that every day all over the world and it happens on ships more time than one would care to believe. It was a heck of way to end out last contract on ships.

The summer ended and we sailed back across the Atlantic to Miami where Daphne and I got off and headed to the suburbs to start a new life. People always ask me if I miss ships or wish to go back and I tell them all the same thing. I loved my time on ships, but I do not miss them at all except for the travel and waking up to a new port. Every Friday I laugh as I know I get my two days off that I never had all those years when working months straight without a day off. I appreciate my life in the suburbs and don't have any itch to go and travel the world, although I do look forward to traveling more when the kids get older.

I hope this book has given you a little glimpse into the life of a crew member. I'm sorry it I wandered at parts of the book, or if some sections were slower than others, but I was trying to do my best to give "context" to the stories as best I could. It has been a fun experience "reliving" my time on ships as I wrote this book and I hope that you have some fun cruise ship stories of your own.

If you have any questions on cruising, how to get a job on a cruise ship, or question about a particular ship, I will be happy to answer them.

You can email me at: guy@cruiseshipstories.com

And don't forget to look me up on Facebook at: https://www.facebook.com/cruiseship.stories

You can check out my photos of life on ships and photos that go along with the stories at my website: http://www.cruiseshipstories.com

Thanks again for reading and if you like the book, please leave a comment on the site where you purchased it, Happy Sailing – Guy Beach

Made in the USA
Middletown, DE
27 March 2024

52141037R10175